I WILL TO YOU

Leaving a Legacy
for Those You *Love*

Herbert Brokering

Augsburg Books

MINNEAPOLIS

I WILL TO YOU
Leaving a Legacy for Those You Love

Unless otherwise marked, scripture quotations are from the New Revised Standard Version Bible, copyright © 1989 by the Division of Christian Education of the National Council of the Churches of Christ in the USA. Used by permission. All rights reserved.

Scripture quotations marked NIV is taken from the Holy Bible, New International Version ®, copyright © 1973, 1978, 1984 International Bible Society. Used by permission of Zondervan Publishing House. All rights reserved.

Unless otherwise identified all hymn texts were written by Herbert Brokering.

Cover photo: Maple leaves, © Achim Sass/Getty Images.
Cover design: Laurie Ingram
Interior design: Michelle L. N. Cook

Library of Congress Cataloging-in-Publication Data
Brokering, Herbert, 1926-
I will to you: leaving a legacy for those you love / by Herbert Brokering.
   p. cm.
ISBN-13: 978-0-8066-5627-4
  ISBN 0-8066-5627-1 (pbk. : alk. paper)
1. Wills, Ethical—Authorship. I. Title.
BJ1286.W6Z82 2006
241—dc22 2006017665

The paper used in this publication meets the minimum requirements of American National Standard for Information Sciences—Permanence of Paper for Printed Library Materials, ANSI Z329.48-1984.

Manufactured in U.S.A.

11   10   09   08   4   5   6   7   8   9   10

Contents

To Mark, Amy, Beth, Jon,

Aya, Chris, Tracy, Evelyn,

Francis, Zoe, Lola, Nathan

I will you this book,

and I will you Earth.

I Will to You

I write this book first of all for you, my family—and then, too, for many readers who, like you, will inherit or who are preparing to make a will.

I have lived long. Eighty years is a lot of life. I have made the legal will. But that is not my only legacy. The garage and basement are filled with shelves, cupboards, and boxes of treasures. I need to get my house in order. Not all my treasures are in boxes. More important is what is in me. On these pages, I give you treasures inside the house that is me.

What can I bequeath you that holds all these things? What one item can I will you that contains all that is mine? Earth! I will you Earth. Earth where you live—your garden, your favorite site: Maui, California, Minnesota, Tokyo—Earth where I live. Any earth. Earth.

In 1970, your mother and I were almost young, and you were very young. On April 22 of that year, Earth Day began. First our country and then the world focused on Earth in a new way. We learned to look at it as a personal gift—as though we had inherited the ground, sea, sun, sky, universe. In Earth, we saw it all. The Earth was holy ground, and Earth Day was a holiday, a celebration, a holy day.

Earth Day morning I drove south to Blue Earth, Minnesota, for a meeting. The air was chilled, some fields were plowed, some grain was planted. I felt good about the name Blue Earth. Earth turned over was deep, deep blue, blue-black. I had been invited to preach at a Communion service. There in the field was the centerpiece, the bouquet, for the communion table—earth. A piece of fresh, old earth. I stopped and lifted one great chunk of dark earth into the car. I can still smell the fresh ground, incense for the table. I drove on with my centerpiece, thinking about the Communion service, planning. It was necessary to revise the sermon (as you know I often have done at the last minute).

Earth is an altar. We live and play and eat and drink and pray and commune and make offerings and celebrate on this

Earth altar. I was driving alone to Blue Earth, and the sermon rewrote itself. Quickly. Perfectly. I hurried to the meeting like a shepherd running to Bethlehem.

I bequeath you Earth—ordinary, extraordinary Earth.

Earth was on the altar in Blue Earth. Bread and wine looked just right beside the bouquet of black earth. I liked the picture with all my heart. It is the picture I knew from my mother's lap—earth as illustrated with woodcuts in my grandfather's big black Bible. Cain and Abel were in the field in worship, and their altar was the earth on which they stood.

We come from earth, we return to earth. Those words, spoken as I have signed the cross with ashes on heads of people, have been the hardest and most blessed of all words. We are born of earth, for the Earth, to earth. The foods and medicines and chemicals of Earth are ours. We need them for life.

I remember making earth pies and tasting them as a child in Nebraska. The earth I tilled and harrowed and plowed and smelled and touched in Nebraska finds its way into most every hymn and poem I write.

Henry Frederick had miracles of earth inside his mother, and he loved the taste of life. He did not taste Mother Earth outside her. But Henry was of earth and returned to the one who created, breathes life into earth.

Lois had Earth life for seventy-five years. She loved being of earth. She dug her hands into earth in gardens and yards and mothered whatever would grow. She wiped dirt from your muddy clothes and faces as though it was an honor.

I will you Earth that carries the seasons you will live: the moods of quiet winter, deep colors and emotions of autumn, expectation and unfolding of spring, and richness and yield of summer. Cold frost, parched heat, fragrant spring, crisp autumn. Earth will give blossoms; Earth will tell you when it's time to plant, to go to the park, to gather in; Earth will rest the woods and gardens. Walk on Earth as though it is yours for a while. Do not miss this day. You have inherited a living Earth. Feed it, for it feeds you. When you pray, look into the sky and over hills and valleys, down at the earth on which you stand. It is true as God said: "Behold, the Earth is very good." So are you.

It was easy to write the hymn, "Earth and All Stars." It, too, is filled with good things of Earth. The stanzas are about what matters on Earth. My hymns and litanies and books are filled with Earth references. You know how much the earth of the Minnesota Valley has shaped our lives and molded our enjoyment. My earth roots are in Nebraska. And I know the earth of Palestine and India and China and Berlin and Krakow and Buchenwald and France and Mexico and Wales and London and Holland. I know the earth Lois and I dug in bombed cathedrals and cities of rubble. I know the earth of cemeteries I mowed as a boy.

Together Lois and I found a hillside where sheep grazed and lambed and cried and cheered us. That Earth place is where I have bought pieces of earth for burial. If you want them, they are yours, too. It is earth near a lake you swam in and fished, a place where sun and picnics helped us grow as family. Sheep have been part of my childhood; their nature has given me words for the *Agnus Dei* ("Lamb of God, who takes away the sin of the world, have mercy on us.") It is good that a Midwestern shepherd's field will be an earthly resting place for me. I also know the one south of Bethlehem. This one is like unto it.

Wherever we lived we planted trees, gave them names. This we did for baptisms, confirmations, Christmases, weddings, Easters, as memorials. Some trees have grown old, some are new. In the earth beneath trees, I have planted shoes I traveled in, poems, haiku, wedding sermons, drawings of children, love notes, little rocks, songs. Earth holds many of my treasures.

It is a sacred piece of property, this Earth you have been given, and only for a while, it is your treasure. Walk gently across it, look twice, be still, listen, make an echo, kiss it, dig it, grow in it, share it. Bless the Earth.

Heaven came to Earth, to earth. You know the song "From Heaven Above to Earth I Come." Jesus did not live long on Earth, but he lived fully. He prayed, "Thy will be done on Earth as it is in Heaven." For me, heaven and Earth are not far apart. You will know more of heaven as you make Earth a friend. In my mind, earth is a means of grace, for earth holds the water, the wine, the bread. Earth held the Way, Truth, Life. Everything came from earth, and all will return to earth. I bequeath you this Earth.

You will find heaven in your way on Earth. Stay close to Earth and close to heaven. They are friends.

I love you all.

Herbert Brokering

Introduction:
Leaving a Living Will

My eightieth birthday is here.

More and more friends and loved ones are passing away. Little ones are being born. The coming and going of time heightens reflection. My thoughts are much with my friends and my loved ones—my children, their children: Evelyn, Henry, Francis, Zoe, Lola, Nathan. Old loved ones, new loved ones. The past, the future.

I also am busy with thoughts of things I want to do in the years ahead, tasks that need putting in order, gifts that need to be handed on. I look around at pieces of my home and my long life and realize there are baskets full of leftovers. Some are only "crumbs," but nevertheless they are "bread," nourishment. When my wife Lois died suddenly in an accident last year, I was left with many precious gifts whose stories I cannot remember alone. What will happen to all these gifts when I am not here? Many will have no meaning without Lois or me. Some will be thrown out and forgotten. Some are unfinished pieces; some are gifts that have never been opened. Some are newborn; others are dear, old friends.

It is time for me to distribute my wealth. Perhaps it is true for you.

WILLS AND THINGS THAT LIVE ON

Not everything of value is covered in a legal document. A legal will is made to take care of big things, concrete matters, property, investments. My children know where my will is. That is not all I have to give. Much of what we cherish most is gathered in small pieces through the years. What about this view of an oak tree outside my window, a song that makes me smile, this dried rose and its memories, last night's compassionate dream? What about the apology I wanted to offer, the thank-you letter I still need to send, the visit I promised to make, the hopes I cherish?

How can I leave these behind?

What will happen to the hymn I started but didn't finish, my ideas for a book or poem not penned? There are sights I have seen and want to share, truths I have discovered, sounds and colors too good to miss.

Through years of teaching and writing, I have stored tubs of notes and writings and artifacts. I could have a party and give them as door prizes. Someone else could take them, use them, hand them on. There are many ways to cherish and share life to the very end and beyond. There are ways to keep parts of ourselves alive even after we are gone.

More than once in the night this idea dawned on me: make another will, a new kind of will. I decided to write my own "living will," bequeathing things that can live on in people I love—my children and grandchildren, relatives and close friends, and those who read my books. Some bequests will be for older people, who can quickly take what I bequeath to do in their mature years. Some are for young persons, who will search in the future for one important thought to have, a compassionate deed to do, a beautiful work to complete. I also have made bequests to people whom I do not know but who will see themselves and understand when they read *I Will to You*.

MAKING A LIVING LEGACY

These "living wills" are not official-looking documents. They are not written in calligraphy, on parchment, or stamped in bronze. They are not long and formal. They are best written the way you write notes and letters—personal, warm, honest—so the reader feels their joy and emotion. They are plain as recipes that need to be understood and used.

Such wills are powerful legacies: possible, worthy, spiritual. They honor the giver and the receiver. And they share the goodness of life, beauty, relationship, love, respect, hope, wonder, faith, grace. The one hundred bequests in this book can be the beginning of a longer list, *your* list to those you love.

The legacies within each of us are important. You can bequeath your own words of forgiveness or thank you or love or wisdom in handwritten notes sealed in envelopes that you address personally. Such bequests don't need to wait for funerals—in fact, they shouldn't. They can be given for holidays, birthdays, and get-well cards.

This book is my legacy of things I want to give and to see live on in people I love. These things are also for you the reader, for strangers, for people everywhere who have in them this unfinished business of living and the dreams that empower us to live as loving children of a loving God.

One hundred is not many. Some of you will have many more bequests of your own. My legacies reach into my early years and my late years; some stretch into the future. If my thoughts stir your own ideas, your own songs, your own legacy, I am thankful. Then I am at peace!

End-of-life matters really matter all of life. Keeping the end in mind helps us to make the journey.

I will you these things. I will you peace!

Herbert Brokering

Favorite Things

"How precious is your steadfast love, O God!" (Psalm 36:7)

"She is more precious than jewels, and nothing you desire can compare with her." (Proverbs 3:15)

"This is the ritual of the grain-offering: The sons of Aaron shall offer it before the Lord, in front of the altar. They shall take from it a handful of the choice flour and oil of the grain-offering, with all the frankincense that is on the offering, and they shall turn its memorial portion into smoke on the altar as a pleasing odor to the Lord." (Leviticus 6:14-15)

Dear God of the morning, you give us our fun,
Old shadows, new gardens, the rain, and the sun;
You send us the robins and flowers in spring.
We give you our praises, our choirs who sing.

We thank you for birthdays, for candles that light,
For snow in the winter, and stars in the night.
May we in the loving we hear and we see
Find God in the heart of our whole family.

You gift wrap the orchards with blossoms in bloom,
Send flower aromas in our living room.
You decorate houses with persons we love;
Keep sending your angels from heaven above.
Hymn: Keep Sending Your Angels
(Augsburg Publishing House)

Bambi

Ah, to live. I will you the book *Bambi*. Three times, I have read the Bambi story: a story with the deer, the forest, and myself. I will you this story that takes you to the heart of a beast. Hear the owl screech her opinion of us. The forest is a mirror. Walk through a woods and hovel to hear nature talk, wondering who will dominate, rape, hunt, and take its life. I will you an hour to read *Bambi* alone, with a child, with someone innocent. Face Earth's great forest and listen, stand vulnerable in an open meadow together, alone. Be a deer for one hour. Feel the dancing of Feline and Bambi in first love, finding, losing, and remembering passion. I will you to know how humans frighten nature to flee, to run, to scatter, to hide, to tremble, and to be alone.

I will you trees and bowing bushes outside your window, beyond your city, in which to roam, to dance, and to hide. I will you the emotion of the owl, the heart of the deer, the want of the red fox, the fallen log, the oak standing, and the bent sagebrush. I will you to walk into a hollow, to lie hid for a while in a hovel, to feel tiny safe spaces of the animal kingdom. I will you the sound of birds warning each other of danger, waking singing with the sun, watching you from hidden perches and high limbs. I will you woods I do not know close-up, deer I only know once in passing, nibbling and watchful, darting, escaping.

You read the news. You know the hiding places. You have read biographies of martyrs, stories of heroes, compassion of mothers. You know door locks, hidden cameras, angelic forces. I will you the compassion of a nursing doe. I will you the pride of a buck with great antlers that walks proudly, leading through danger. I will you a deer, God's beast, graying, alone, having lived long, escaped, fading, wise, mentor of a fawn. I will you your turn for a slow walk into your own forest, watchful, listening. I will you to know the heart and soul of Bambi wanting to live.

"As a deer longs for flowing streams,
so my soul longs for you, O God." (Psalm 42:1)

Hoop and Stick

Our home was simple. That means we used anything in lots of ways; we did not have many things. I have long liked the song "'Tis a Gift to Be Simple." Simplicity brings a kind of freedom.

I remember the freedom and fun of an iron hoop and a stick. So, I will you something simple, like a hoop and a stick, of willow or elm or oak or pine. I will you a single stick, a friend, and a hoop. An iron hoop and a three-foot stick to push and steer the hoop. That was all we needed to be happy, ecstatic: a stick and a hoop. I will you a simple thing that will make you glad.

We ran and laughed, focused and felt proud to keep the iron hoop rolling, even on a broken sidewalk. Soon we could turn corners without stopping, go very fast, faster, and run. Going slow was hardest to keep the hoop from wobbling down and stop rolling. I will you the gift to play fast and slow with something simple: a hoop and stick. We laid the stick between two poles to jump over into a pile of soft ground. It was really very simple: one stick balanced precariously on two uprights with nails. I will you a stick and two nails, soft earth, and a friend.

What do you use in many different ways? What is your simple gift? The same stick took us fishing. A line, a hook, a grasshopper, and sitting still beside a creek. I will you a stick and a string and hope; hope is the greatest of these three. In spring, we stuck the stick into the ground at the end of a long row for planting potatoes. A stone on one end, a stick on the other, and a string made the straight line. I will you a stick and a line in a garden. The stick took us into the pasture. If the stick was smooth, we wrapped five hundred feet of string around it to unravel slowly or swiftly when flying a kite. If the wind was strong, two of us held the one stick to fly a homemade kite into a high open sky. I will you a simple smooth stick, five hundred feet of strong string, and a high sky.

What have you used so each time it needs a new name? God made us to look at one thing from all sides. You have this gift. I will the simple joy of a stick and a string, a hoop and a stick, a stick and a garden. I will you something simple to enjoy with a friend.

Soft Lead Pencil

I liked a #3 lead pencil in country school. I never drew in ink. Writing in ink was something I'd use in the final writing. Ink was like going to press. There could be no more changes. I liked the lead pencil, so soft that I could not hear it while writing or drawing. The feeling of #3 lead was the feeling of the pencil and the paper talking to each other. They were friendly. I could make a mistake and feel forgiven.

I bequeath you the art of friendly writing, feeling in touch with each of your words. The lead would allow you to erase. With a soft erasure, it will not smear. You can start over and not leave a mark.

So, what I wrote did not corner me. I was not afraid to write or draw, for my word and lines and shades were not final. If the leg of a horse I drew was too short, I could lengthen it. I remember drawing in ink. The beak of a duck was crooked. I remember the feeling of trying to straighten it in ink. That was seventy years ago. I have the picture of the duck; the beak is both crooked and straight. I drew Joe Lewis in pencil. His muscles became mine. I will you a #3 pencil. In the days before computers and spell-check, a #3 lead pencil helped me start right in with writing. I could always make a change.

A boy in the next seat in school would spend ten minutes waiting, afraid to make the first mistake. He did not like writing and drawing. He sat in school afraid to misspell, afraid to make a wrong line on an art project. He could not begin. I had a hard time stopping. He used the eraser more than I did. Writing and drawing were like flying over mountains, through valleys, in the sky for me. Words flowed on and on.

My father drove fast. He started fast, drove fast, and stopped fast. There is a #3 lead pencil inside me; I started fast. I will you the fun of getting started fast. Enjoy the flow of thinking, feeling, writing, drawing, and knowing you can make changes later. Editing can wait. I will you the free spirit I felt in Greenfield country school enjoying the soft lead of a #3 pencil.

Music

Music is all around. You have practiced, performed, listened. I had a few piano and violin lessons from my father. I wanted to play, but when I learned it meant I had to practice, I quit. Alas! I dug a hole and buried a talent. How do you do music? Perhaps you play a horn or sing in a choir, are a good listener, attend concerts, encourage others to play and sing. I bequeath you many ways to do music.

Through the years, I have learned to collaborate with many musicians. Combo groups have played the emotions of my story telling. Guitars of children have helped campers feel woods and nights and winds I described in poetry. Lois made my poems sound better with her background music. Orchestras and choirs harmonized minutes of national conventions that I set to rhyme. Music is not something to do alone. You have heard flutes and oboes in the wind. You have felt drums in the vibration of windowpanes in winter. You know the beating drums in horses cantering and galloping, and the music in sirens. You have heard timpani in thunderstorms and clashing of cymbals with lightning. I will you the sounds of nature and the music of silence.

In a musical journey to Norway, I wrote essays on musical markings. Listen and look what there is in Legato. "I am Legato. I am smooth. I slide as on ice, move through air currents. I glide at any altitude. I sail a sea of words without making ripples. My wings are not heard in flight. Every movement is from inside out. I am at peace with each consonant and vowel and know the space of a preposition. I know the power of each verb, the self inside a noun. I see a soul inside its word. I sing a song to feel a smooth rush, to travel a straight line of power. I am Legato; sometimes I waltz, sometimes I swing. I float; sometimes I hang loose, a green willow in quiet summer, barely moving. I am a baby breathing sleeping. I am smooth as breath, automatic, even, life flowing, unending."

You know the meaning of Crescendo. "I am Crescendo. I am increasing. I open like a bud into full bloom. My petals unfold and fill me. I am a fountain slowly, surely flooding to the brim. I will hold no more. I am the roar of a wind coming from a distance, arriving full force. There is no room for more. I am Crescendo. I am the steady waking of a new day. I am the light breaking into dark and waking the horizon from east to west into one full white light. I fill sky with my breath. I am a full wave reaching a great height. I know the deep of a sea and rise up wave on wave on wave. I am Crescendo; I wake like dawn, swell like pride, open to a bloom, fill a phrase with full foliage. I am fulfilled."

Dave Brubeck learned jazz from a California water pump, a gallop and canter of a horse, and a good teacher. I bequeath you to find your music in the world around you.

Train

I memorized a train whistle seventy years ago. I will you a train whistling in the distance. A train you cannot see but hear coming softly, loudly, disappearing into the horizon. I will you the whistle of one train that sings the same song. You know the time of day of one train, always on time in the night, in the morning. A train is my distant friend. I will you a train whistle to feel sound moving, life passing by, from long ago. I hear one train I did not see when I was nine, but heard. I still find that whistle in every train I hear near and far off. Listen to a train whistle taper into silence and waken a train sound you know from the past. Find your train, foghorn, sound.

When I was six, I lay my ear to the track to hear a train coming miles before its whistle. I felt the vibrato in the rail—no sound—only the quiver of a drum in the iron rails. I will you a train in the distance, coming from a distance, coming closer. At dusk I often waved, felt the coal smoke like a cloud from which a voice said my name: the word of the engineer. In the dark I still wave, feel a train far off. I lie in bed remembering coming and going, thinking last year and tomorrow. I will you the five minutes a train whistle clocks time, appears and disappears, a metronome singing its way on iron wheels. I will you the whistle of a train you once heard and will hear wherever there is a train blowing a song, a tune that lives inside you like music: an instrument of puffing sound, a blast of steam, a clicking on iron rails, and a disappearing. I will you sounds of iron music that waken your spirit to times long past, strong sounds, still moving by, coming and going.

I will you an old sound that sounds new when there's a whistle blowing, which you cannot see: a ship at sea, an oboe, a band on main street, your old car, the Shofar horn of Israel, the trumpet at Easter, a bell. You know the power of nostalgia. I bequeath an old voice that wakens deep good feelings.

A Cow

I knew when I was thirteen I knew her well. I will you knowing one animal well, by heart. Father bid on her at a sale. He knew how to judge a milk cow. She cost nineteen dollars and fifty cents. I was proud that father, a preacher, understood cows and chose well. We waited to see if she was good as father believed. Betsy was.

I will you studying carefully one cow, or horse or cat or bird, to understand it close-up. Betsy was Holstein and Guernsey. I liked that she carried two ancestors in her. Farmers around us talked about our cow, and agreed this would be a good cow for a preacher's family. They talked about cream, cream tests, and milk volume. I expected her to do what they said. She did more. Each time I milked, I expected a lot, for I knew her potential.

I will you knowing the potential of one cow or bird or person. I will you to know the animal at its best. She knew us, each voice in the dark, and a call from a distance. At dusk she came slowly to the barn with heavy udder ready for milking. She was gifted, generous, and gracious. We treated her like a member of the family. I will you being good to one gifted, generous animal.

I felt her warm breath in cold mornings, heard her stomachs rumble as I milked. I pictured the miracle of her seven stomachs, each busy, each taking its turn inside her. She chewed cud to a rhythm. I sang to the rhythm. The more I sang the more milk she gave, and father agreed. I sang hymns of the church, she chewed and breathed deeply, and I was as in church. Sitting on a homemade milk stool was like sitting in a front pew and the organ playing softly. Milking time was special. My head rested against the miracle inside her as she munched hay and grain, gave us milk and cream, and sweet butter. I thought of water turning to wine, green grass becoming white milk. How warm her milk, how sweet, how much, how special.

I will you finding a miracle in one cow, one cat, one beast, one bird, one butterfly. I memorized the aroma of her skin, and the aroma of hay and breath. I knew her world. I will you a close-up of a cow, a canary, a rabbit, a lamb. Milking was often my chore, an honor. I can feel sixty years ago, the warmth, the air, the aroma of sweet milk. I rehearsed her birth, her youth, her calf, her old age.

I will you the lifeline of a cow, a cat, one creature you know for a long while, like family. I will you the family of creation: creatures, birds of the air, one sparrow, one lamb, one rose bush, and one Spruce. I will you knowing one cow, one bird, one creature very well.

Wood

Each day I sit at an oak desk. The grain has the rhythm and color of a seashore. The grains in the wood are like markings of waves reshaping sand. I pretend to be sitting on a beach, watching the motion of an ocean and hearing the sound of waves quiet in this one piece of oak wood. I see a piece of oak wood and am in awe of a beach. I will you wood that takes your mind to a seashore.

Near me is a wooded valley that has talked to our family for years. It speaks in Japanese. I hear a mother's voice to her children in the time of World War II: "Tomorrow we go home." We found a pile of boards buried in the Minnesota Valley where Japanese families were interned during the war. Their houses were in this valley beside a river and a lake. Cement blocks still mark the borders of rooms. Trees sixty years old are growing out of what were kitchens and bedrooms. For years, I took pieces of this wood to schools. Children cocked their ears to hear the words of a Japanese mother: "Tomorrow we go home." The *Japanese wood* held them to the story. I will you a piece of wood with a true story. What are the wood stories you know?

We took youth to the Savage city dump to watch the unloading. One rocking chair was thrown from a truck by a man whose family was done with it. The rocking chair was discarded. We rescued the chair, not because we needed it as much it needed a home. Under seven coats of paint, Lois found the wood. We set the chair under the sun. After many years, the wood of the chair and the sun met again. When quiet, we heard the soft words of admiration between the two, for the sun had grown the wood. They were back together. The chair is now in our kitchen. We have studied and cherished the chair as an artifact. When we sit and rock, we hear the woman who rocked and hummed babies to sleep. I will you a chair of wood rescued, restored, rocking.

You know pieces of wood: chairs, tables, wood toys, favorite lumber, pine with knots and aroma of pine. You know the circles and markings of years of growth and rainfalls revealed in cross-cuts of wood. You know the reason for knots in boards, their limbs that once held nests and swings of children. I bequeath you a piece of wood that helps you hear ocean waves, a Japanese mother, a bird singing on a limb, or a rabbi on a hill calling seven great sentences from a tree.

Dining Table

What is the value of an old dining room table? I will you a dining room table that hosted our family for four decades. The table is like new if you remove four coats of varnish and sand it properly. You will find tiny markings pressed into the wood from children drawing and doing homework.

I will you a table that for forty years had centerpieces for supper of every season: Christmas, Epiphany, Easter, Pentecost, Halloween, Thanksgiving, and birthdays. I will you the table with its yellow chalk marks "Jon" underneath. Children played under the table, laughed around the table, sat in their same chairs at the table. At the table, we bowed heads, said fast prayers, explained things. I will you table manners, table talks, and favorite casseroles.

You know such a table. You know the markings and moods of an old favorite table. I will you a table where you hear what happened in the day, who got hurt, how it feels to be chosen, what it's like to lose. I will you a table that cost twenty-five dollars forty years ago and was found in the Salvation Army store on Fourth Avenue. I will you a used table that was like new to a young family, forty years ago, varnished four times for scuffs and made waterproof for spilled milk and hot chocolate. I will you the shining surface, lighted from overhead for writing term papers or for feeling near the family when night comes. I will you the table that was manufactured in North Carolina.

I will you candles in the center of cherry wood and yellow daffodils facing every direction, decorating a simple supper of soup and salad, and many peanut butter sandwiches. I will you food and drink and friends and family at a used dining table. This table has found a new home; it was priceless, so we gave it to someone who would prize it. You have a table you are making priceless.

> "People will come from east and west, from north and south,
> and will eat in the kingdom of God." (Luke 13:29)

Aroma

In graduate school, I learned that as a newborn I recognized my mother by aroma. If skin smelled like anyone else, I no doubt cried or squirmed until Mother held me. I will you the miracle of aroma.

Homemade bread was why I hurried home from country school on Mondays. The smell of honey on warm bread has not left my mind. Tuesdays in the winter, I came home to smell wash hanging in the kitchen, drying in the warmth. The sweet smell of fresh laundry filling a winter room is in me. I know the smell of country air when opening the door of our home's north parlor. The room was not heated, and a breath of that air was a taste of winter in our wood-heated house.

For ten days, I guided a group of young people through what was East Germany. At the end, we told what we had discovered. One student remembered every site and city by aromas. The scent of chimneys and bakeries and factories and peasants and barns and cars and food and flowers and pollution and cathedrals outlined his journey.

Aroma. The offerings of God's people. Burnt offerings, incense, coals, spices to please God. Perfumes as signs of adoration. I will you the aroma of Bethlehem—the incense of the cave, the nativity site, the smell of animals and hay, the earth. The smell of adoration is there. You will take the gift. You know how to close your eyes and drink the air. You will welcome smells of food to cover your table, the taste and aroma of each dish. I will you the beauty of aromas you know and ones that are new: new homes, new rooms, new gardens, new trees, new flowers. There is the aroma of sickness and healing, of books, of seasons, of communion, of Good Friday and Easter. There is the aroma of war and peace, of old age and of birth. I will you the aromas of life.

Sparrow House

I made a birdhouse with men and women in graduate school. It was my assignment to theology students in Ohio. "This semester we will also build a sparrow house." I brought the wood to the class in a paper bag. Each week they had trouble beginning to build a sparrow house. This was a graduate course; they snickered at the assignment. Who wants to build a sparrow house for credit? I will you that sparrow house built for credit. I will you to do something common for credit.

Finding the word *sparrow* in scripture made a big difference. Suddenly, *sparrow* was a word like *God*. The theology students began to bring sparrow songs, information, stories to class. They talked about sparrows, and those who are poor, outcast, lonely. They agreed sparrows are not always loved, and yet sparrows sing. I will you to hear the singing of those who are poor. I will you chirping songs of sparrows.

Twelve men and women in Ohio painted the sparrow house blue, put a cross over the door, and were satisfied. They loved the sparrow house by the tenth week of class. You know how a common place or task can feel big. An old chair can become a favorite. I will you the common sparrow house with a cross built by seminary students.

At the end of the course, they gave me the bright blue sparrow house. I willed it to prisoners in a retreat who felt the sparrow's song as common as its feathers and felt the reputation of a sparrow: fallen. They wanted the house. The warden said it was not allowed. So, the prisoners studied it. They closed their eyes to remember it, to take it into their prison rooms with their eyes. They each took the one house with the sparrow, with the chirping songs. I will you the sparrow house in thirty rooms of five Wisconsin prisons.

The blue sparrow house came to be known by many. It stood in the chancel of a cathedral, went to conventions, and was borrowed by a halfway house. In the night, the halfway house burned, and the bright blue sparrow house with it. I will you ashes of the sparrow house, the quilts, clothing, and paper bags of those who are poor. I will you the sparrow story to waken your love for those who are poor, outcast, oppressed. I will you the sparrow house that outlives fire in this story in you. I bequeath you what is common, to have life and to live.

"Are not two sparrows sold for a penny? Yet not one of them will fall to the ground unperceived by your Father." (Matthew 10:29)

Little Rock

Tim was graduating from high school. What gift could I give? He had everything, except a rock from the Mediterranean. Years before, we brought this one stone from the great sea. In it were buried the lives and deeds of apostles, and what made the land holy from the sea side, the west side. These waters took the good news into the uttermost parts of the earth.

We willed Tim a rock from the waters of the Mediterranean, just off the shore of Caesarea Philippi. We willed him a rock we found, studied, loved, kept, cherished, and gave away. The rock is sculpted by water and wind and powers of the sea. It has a hundred sides, bent, curved, smooth.

I am sure you cherish something ordinary and then make it special. It becomes special when you finally give it away. We willed Tim this rock from where Jesus walked, where Paul boarded a ship, where Caesar built aqueducts and shrines. The world is full of rock stories.

Lois once saw a little boy covered with mud examining a rock closely. She heard Nate say: "Little rock, where have you been?" That tiny moment grew into her song:

> Little rock, little rock, where have you been?
> Little rock, little rock, tell me what you've seen.
> When the earth was hot and new,
> where were you, rock, where were you?
> Little rock, little rock, where have you been?
> —*Lois Brokering*

The song has been sung in hundreds of places by thousands of children and parents. It has been arranged for choirs. It was tiny and muddy when she saw it and heard the boy. It is not a little thing to bequeath a little rock. Nate has the tiny rock from the Great Sea. Find Nate and you will find the rock.

I wrote a poem for the rock from the Great Sea. I gave the rock and poem to Tim in my old sock. The rock and my sock are on his journey of faith along some great sea where Tim now walks by faith. In the sock is a note to help him listen to the rock:

I am a rock, washed by waters of the great sea, carved by waves on every side, pounded by waves and storms, shaped by high winds, formed and reformed by a spirit and breath that breathed into all stone and air and waters, and one voice said: let there be. I am not any other rock, or the shape of any other spirit, for I have been covered and freed by the only one who gives birth and rebirth in the blink of an eye or eons on eons, which is the same to God the rock.

"Trust in the Lord *for ever, for in the* Lord God *you have an everlasting rock." (Isaiah 26:4)*

Church Bells

Surely you love bells. So, I will you bells I know; I will you your own. What bells do you know best?

The thick rope in the corner of the Long Branch church hung loose, a knot tied at the end, a rope worn smooth after sixty years of ringing. I will you a rope of a church bell that rings through the countryside, a message heard in houses, barns, and hay fields, and over children shouting handy-handy-over. The ringing was the fun, the pulling, the power of the swinging bell, the clanging, and the rhythm. All these at once made ringing a church bell an honor. And then there was the message.

I will you the message of the ringing bell, Saturday night in the country, at dusk ringing to remind farm people of Sabbath in the morning. Chores ran late; Sabbath was almost beginning. Bells filled the evening air with holy sounds. I will you the beginning of Sabbath, preparing for a holy time, for shalom. Then came early Sunday bells: ringing, swinging, singing. Time to finish chores, to dress, Sunday shoes, to church on time, the right pew, the same seat, in time for singing. I will you the ringing of bells with the big rope, hanging loose, tied to one ton of sacred steel, with a Bible verse printed all the way around. I bequeath you the sound of being called to worship.

And I will you the other rope, the small rope hanging high, a tiny knot, a rope not so worn as the big rope. The thin rope, the bell for tolling, tolling, tolling, tolling the number of years of the dead, and tolling threefold during the Lord's Prayer. I will you the sound of the tolling bell that leads people over hills, through cornfields, in rain to a hilltop, to a grave side, under a green tent set against a cold wind, with the aroma of flowers—black veils and suits and believers in awe of resurrection. I will you believing the resurrection and life everlasting with the tolling of the clapper by the thin rope. I will you the long Sabbath, the swinging, ringing, singing of a country bell, the big rope for now, and the little rope for eternity.

There are two ways to ring a bell, the thick rope and the thin rope. I bequeath you to know them both. There will always be these two ropes to ring the big bell.

Baptismal Font

Being baptized is a constant strength in me. Baptism blankets me with a comfort beyond my understanding.

The fonts I know are many. They are a river, a kitchen bowl in New York, a marble font in Minnesota, a stone font in Eisenach, a paper cup in San Antonio, a shower, a fountain in an Iron Curtain country. They are all different; they are all the same. The font is where I am declared a member of the world, the universe, of heaven and Earth, and so a child of God. I will you a font; one spot on Earth with water, a word and a sign that everything is one. All children on one journey, all breathing the same spirit, all God's family, all hollering "Help," all in need of being loved, all children of God.

Last week I baptized Kathy, age eight days. I gave her socks from Cambodia and China and the words: "You are now a member of the world. All these from all nations are now your sisters and brothers." The font was truly a globe.

I will you the font: a paper cup, a seashell, a marble bowl, a silver dish, the palm of a hand. I will you the one water that is all water, the one word of all words. I will you the sign of the cross that declares you will live, love, suffer, die, and rise. I bequeath you to belong to this family of God. With my eye on the font, I wrote a poem for a dedication. The reading was accompanied by elegant dancing while a bell choir played.

> I am the font, the river of life, the Jordan, the river that flows to the Lamb. I am the water of Galilee, soaked through the high mountain of Hermon, snow capped by rains of all nations, running into a sea called Galilee. I am the font, the river of life, where the healing journey of Jesus is marked on the brow, in the sign of the cross, forever. I am the wet walk that never dries, that reminds children and old, in every step and walk of life, "You are beloved." I am the voice from above, "You are my own. I have called you by my name." I am the font, where all in every place and time have one family name, the name of God. I am the font.

The Cross

I will you the cross. On one wall in our house are hung eighteen crosses brought from many parts of the world. I will you one cross in your house as a sign of "the cross." Often, when stretching my arms out, I view my body as being the cross. Ceilings in the house and lines in ceramic tiles are signs of the cross. I have heard children discover them and shout: "Crosses, crosses, crosses!" I will you to see crosses in ordinary places.

On the highest tower in what was East Berlin, the sun marked a cross every day. Attempts to prevent the sign were foiled. I will you a cross in sunlight and night light, under stars, moon, and clouds. I saw a clown in an act beat someone into the ground, wounded, until the outstretched arms of a crouched clown remained as the image of a cross. I will you to feel the suffering of people oppressed and beaten. A cross of mirrors set up in a German city square reflected traffic, busses, cars, people on cycles, and shoppers as they passed. I saw myself *in* the cross, looking out; I saw the whole world passing by.

In worship, I often mark the cross on myself when the name of Christ is spoken. I will you to remember you are marked with the sign of the cross forever and there are ways to hold that truth before your face. Some of my friends bow at the name of Jesus, modestly showing reverence for the grace given them. Sometimes bow, if not outwardly then inside.

St. Paul speaks of being crucified with Christ. This I bequeath you: to know that what Christ endured you can endure, and what Christ was willing to redeem you are willing to risk saving. We are able to do heroic deeds. This is a high calling. Once at Christmas in a camp, I tied a cross to my back and entered the room. The youth were fascinated, and finally agreed. The greatest gift we have in the manger is the Christ who will carry every hurt and injustice and evil in the world and feel how it feels. In this way they heard the words Mary sang in the Magnificat. When my friend was dying, I marked a large cross on her as she lay there. She smiled and said, "Mmmm." She knew the hymn, "In the Cross of Christ I Glory." She knew that we who die and are buried with Christ will also be "raised with him."

All this is in the cross story, in the cross. I often mark the cross on people thousands of miles away, on airplanes overhead, on battlefields I will never see, on plants budding, and on white-out storms in winter with travelers finding their paths. When I bequeath you the cross, I will you God's good will.

"[We look to] Jesus the pioneer and perfecter of our faith, who for the sake of the joy that was set before him endured the cross, disregarding its shame, and has taken his seat at the right hand of the throne of God." (Hebrews 12:2)

Places to Be

"Jesus went throughout Galilee, teaching in their synagogues and proclaiming the good news of the kingdom and curing every disease and every sickness among the people. So his fame spread throughout all Syria, and they brought to him all the sick, those who were afflicted with various diseases and pains, demoniacs, epileptics, and paralytics, and he cured them. And great crowds followed him from Galilee, the Decapolis, Jerusalem, Judea, and from beyond the Jordan." (Matthew 4:23-25)

Come, walk up the mountain, the hillside is steep.
The blossoms love springtime; the newborn will leap.
The mountain is covered with sunshine and warm.
The desert will bloom and my heart be reborn.

Come, walk through the city, the walls tumble down.
Cathedrals need candles; the world needs a crown.
The city is waking with angels around.
The desert will bloom through cement in the ground.

Come, walk through the nations, the warring will cease.
The swords will be plowshares; the songs will increase.
The desert is turning like water to wine.
The desert will bloom like a fruit on the vine.
Hymn: The Desert Will Bloom
(Augsburg Publishing House)

Swing

What is there about the swing? It was so much like flying: feet off the ground, wind blowing past face and hair, heading into sky and clouds, and then back for one more ride, and again and again, a little higher, faster, more daring. There are times when feet must leave the ground. I will you times with feet off the ground. You will not fall.

And there is the swing on the porch, in the shade during summer heat, in the sun on cool evenings. This restful swing does not go into the wild blue yonder; this swing helps you ponder, remember, feel the setting sun, the evening cool, the morning dew. I will you the swing that rocks, barely moves. In this swing, all times meet and your body feels like a quiet metronome. The heartbeat and meter of the swing meet, and a song comes to mind: a face, a time past, a wish, a dream, a thanksgiving. Feel the rhythm of was and will be, past and future, and being here and now. In this swing, being is enough.

I will you a strong rope with a large knot on the end to carry you off the side of a hill, over water, looking down into a valley, too high to jump or fall. I will you hanging on with both hands. You know how to hold on, stay tight, be sure, swing over a deep place, and make it.

You are not finished with swings. You are not done swinging where feet cannot touch the earth. I will you the spirit of holding on. Look into the distance if looking down is frightening. Feel the strong rope holding you. Feel the rocking you felt when newborn, being held and loved, the humming of someone saying your name over and over. I will you the joy of swings.

Cupola

A cupola sat high on the Peterson barn for over one hundred years. From there, one could see over Coleman Lake and the Minnesota River south into Scott County. Children must have climbed there often to see the world where Dakota and Sioux tribes once pitched their tents, hunted and rode the river, sang, danced. I will you a high place where you can climb, look in all directions, feel the world turning slowly like a merry-go-round. I will you a high place to see over a valley and river and grain elevators where wigwams and canoes and bonfires reigned a hundred years ago. I will you to see history from high places, to see what was, will be, and is.

Everyone looks in all directions, and from some place high above. Where do you climb to see far?

I will you looking farther than you can see standing where you are. I know you too like vistas and hilltops from which to see and dream. Who doesn't have an aerial view? I will you a river whose water runs beyond where you can see from the cupola, flowing from a trickle in Itasca downhill to be the Mississippi River and into the Gulf of Mexico. I will you a cupola where, sitting with a friend, the view steals your breath as you know what eagles feel. I will you the tips of oak trees in September, the fresh yellow green coloring of willows in April, and cornfields in bloom. I will you looking from a high cupola into all seasons, all directions, and all times gone and coming. I will you a cupola slowly rusting, alone, needing care and one more climb to take a look.

The cupola outlived farmer Peterson, rhythmic sun dances of Sioux in the valley, and the hillside of mighty oak. The Peterson barn is gone, white houses stand in its place, the cupola no longer sees sunrises. I will you the quiet cupola, standing silent one hundred feet from my window, rusting but resting on a hillside it once saw from above. Hear the breathing of the cupola. I will you the quiet breath of a cupola that outlives the loft of hay, a grain bin, one silo, and Mr. Peterson. I bequeath high places to climb where you see from above.

Cellar

Think of the wonder of being underground. I know many cellars. The ones I know best have the aroma of potatoes stored through the winter and apples wrapped in paper and kept fresh as possible for winter eating. I still know the aroma of the limestone walls, earth floor, and the smell of underground things. Here is where we went in storms, went to choose canned meats and vegetables from September canning in the kitchen. Here is the smell of homemade root beer brewing, and shelves of pickles and carrots and peas looking as fresh as when they were picked and pulled in the garden. I will you the earthy and delicious aroma of a fruitful cellar.

We hurried into the cellar when tornadoes and twisters came across the fields. There we were safe. We prayed and sang songs until the storm passed by or over. The cellar was the ark in which we huddled in dark for safety. Father was the first to lift the cellar door and declare the good news. I will you a safe place where with others you can huddle and feel safe in a storm-filled Earth.

You remember a cool cellar in hot days. There with dim light we could imagine the mystery of gophers and moles and snakes living safe and cool in their earthen homes. In the cellar we could join all reptiles that left the hot sun and slithered silently into their houses for refuge. The Earth has an underside. I bequeath you the underside of Earth, where roots find their drink and animals find their nests and we find shelves of canned foods, drinks, and fresh fruits. You know alleys where looking down into cellars you see food and drink moving up and down the stairs. Cities are filled with cellars.

There are natural cellars: caverns, caves, and canyons. You dug earth when little, played with sand, made mud pies, and found underground holes. You know the dark cracks in thirsty earth, the mystery of a closed mine, a cave growing mushrooms. I bequeath you cellars and caves and places of refuge inside Mother Earth. Immigrants made early homes under the earth. I will you the safety and marvel of Mother Earth.

"The earth is the Lord's *and all that is in it." (Psalm 24:1)*

Russian Olive

I know a Russian olive tree on the north side of the house. Winter winds were cold, and rags in windowsills kept drapes in the north bedroom hanging quiet. The sound of the north wind beat on the windows like waves of a timpani, and the rattle was like a visitor from North Pole.

I will you the north side of a winter room in a storm. Inside we were safe. This year we believed the years ahead would be better. The reason: Russian olive trees. Father had planted twelve Russian olive trees in a row thirty feet from the house, the north side. Russian olive was a new phrase in our household. It was bred to be the first tree in line against cold in a country hedgerow.

I bequeath you safety in a storm, being comforted, being better off than before. You know the times you were warmer, safer, more loved, and calmer. I bequeath you times that feel like a row of trees to protect you from a storm.

Do you remember the storms? Winds blew, the olive green leaves hung on branches for dear life; the new trees caught blowing wet snow and held it. In the north bedroom, I was grateful for the new immigrant tree, the Russian olive.

I will you a brand-new tree that gives you hope: a friend, a neighbor, a church that shelters you in a storm. In winters, mother promised us the quilt would be warm; there were more for when the sun went down into the dark. Father promised the Russian olive trees would protect us from the north. They were still little, and they would grow. We slept under quilts and twelve Russian olive trees were at our side. I will you signs of protection in the night, in the cold, in long nights.

I grew; years passed. In a North Dakota town, I met a boy who showed me eleven rows of trees protecting the north side of his farm. I do not remember the names of the eleven trees. I know the name of the first row, the north row that stands against the cold wind. Trent said, "That's the Russian olive." He felt warm and safe. You know the feeling. I will you a row of trees that make you safe. You know what makes you warm, safe. The song "Safe in the Arms of Jesus" has kept me warm in many cold times.

Cemetery

I walk different on a cemetery than on a playground. When I was a country boy, preachers' kids often mowed the church cemetery. I did this with my brother and sisters. It was often hot on the hill, but the country wind made it all worthwhile. It was an honor to walk among the graves of old and young and feel stories and lives under my boy feet. I mowed with respect. I bequeath you a regard for the dead.

When new graves sank, I pretended not to stare as relatives filled in the caved-in sections. I mowed so they could work through their feelings alone; these were sacred times and I thought of Ash Wednesday when my father said over and over: "We came from dust and we will return to dust." Dust was earth and that is the wonderful way God has wrapped our spirits into a human form. I will you respect for earth and dust.

Mowing the paths between graves was like walking hallways of a biblical museum. The gravestones were not alike. A few were wood, their words and shape simple. Most were crosses. Some were bent; years of rain and wind shaved some of the letters. I stopped often to decipher words no longer in clear print. The stone was soft; I am sure the family could not afford marble or bronze. One marker was five cement logs piled on top of each other—five children from one family. In each mowing, I moved slowly past the words: "Our dear five angels." I felt their hurt without knowing the real story. I bequeath you respect for ordinary saints with simple markers—wood crosses, soft stone, or cement—their symbols and words worn.

I mowed fast past marble stones with large print and Bible verses spelled out in two languages. Their ornate flowers, leaves, and doves were as clear as the gold details of our country altar. A family was generous, honoring a loved one. These grey and red marble stones stood like cathedrals on the hilltop and made the verses truer out in the open than they felt inside the Bible.

You have learned to honor and respect saints and heroes of faith. Whether young or old, it is the way we were raised. You too walk slowly through spaces where the dead sleep. I will you a place where those under your feet make you strong, still, respectful.

Holy Place

Altars can bring me close to God, whether marble, plywood, ornate, magnificent and gilded, a table, or a cardboard box with a towel. The altar centers my worship. How is it with you? An altar can be the focus of the people who meet: the altar or table with white parament, candles, a book, some bread with a cup, a sign of faith.

What makes a place holy for worship? An altar, a river, a walk, a friend, a wood, a meadow, a mountain, a meal, a need?

Jerry, a priest, described his holy place to twenty chaplains. With his hands and imagination, he gathered five hundred rocks, and in this chapel room in Newport, Rhode Island, created an altar. Jerry is an Irish immigrant chaplain. The rocks he described were from Ireland and ten countries he knows by heart: stones touched by oceans, some birthed from volcanoes, some washed by waterfalls, some tumbled from mountains, some crushed by the ice age. I will you one altar made of many stones. Jerry shaped five hundred stones into one altar. He held them, prayed they would stay put, and made them all fit. I will you Jerry who labored to make a place more holy with stones.

Jerry the priest finished arranging the stones and leaned back as though done.

I asked him to kiss the holy place. He kissed the front left corner, to him most holy. His lips, he said, were kissing a stone from Jerusalem. We were silent. Jerry kissed the stone once more. His lips, he explained, touched a relic in the stone. Pressed against the stone, his spirit found a martyr. I will you Jerry who cares for strong believers who will lay down life. Again, Jerry pressed his lips against the relic, saying he was in the catacombs of Rome, in the early church, underground, in a holy place with saints. His kiss was the passing of peace in Holy Communion. I will you joining Jerry in the sacred passing of peace. Once more, he kissed the rock of his holy altar. He said: "My lips are kissing Christ." There was no more to do. Jerry the priest was home.

Then Jerry gave us the kiss of peace; we passed it on to each other. Three thousand pounds was the weight of one altar. What looked like a pile of stone was the passing of peace. Twenty chaplains were in awe. Captain Bill, a Baptist with tears, said, "Jerry, I have a holy place like this too." Bill hummed: "On a hill far away stood an old rugged cross." I will you Bill's song and the corner of Jerry's altar where he went to kiss Christ. I will you a holy place where you can find your way to God.

Hobo Angels

I met angels every night that I prayed. In my long night prayer, angels filled the room. Their spears of gold were God's own word. I will you prayers of angels.

Who was your first angel? The first real angels I knew were in rags. They came to our house from nearby train tracks where trains stopped. Men in rags and smelly clothes rode the trains looking for work, food, shelter, hope. They always found our house, worked a while for father, sweat, and earned their bread. I remember the first angel. He entered our kitchen and stood beside mother as she prepared his food. Mother made three sandwiches, two sandwiches for the hobo angel; one sandwich was for me. We sat side by side, on the porch steps, quiet, and ate. I will you eating with an angel.

This angel was tired, clothes worn, hair uncombed. Each time a hobo came, father whispered, "This could be an angel of the Lord, the way angels sat at Abraham and Sarah's tent." I believed this could be a real angel next to me, facing south, on the parsonage steps, eating a peanut butter sandwich. I will you sitting with an angel, sweaty, silent, and eating. The train he came on had gone. I knew the pile of ashes where a hobo would make a fire to stay warm, cook in a tin can, then lie under a blanket to sleep. An aluminum can was the angel's water cup, for angels came poor.

Today, they are not named *hobos*. They are *unemployed, transient, disenfranchised, street persons*. They no longer knock on doors. It is hard for angels in rags to get to your front porch. The angels who sat beside me eating sandwiches had something I understood. They were hungry, they were quiet, they were thankful, and they didn't know much about tomorrow. I felt the same. My first angel in rags was younger than mother, had good teeth, said he was out of work, and did not complain. Mother felt sorry. I will you an uncomplaining angel.

In the Bible, Jacob didn't know where he was going. One night, he saw angels going up and down a ladder between heaven and the ground. I will you an angel that takes you between earth and heaven. When the sandwiches were eaten, my first angel left to catch the next train. Near sunset, I saw him climb an iron ladder that went straight to the top of a red boxcar. He lay down so no one would see him. When an engine hooked onto the car, he sat up, looked back, waved, and looked ahead. I will you an angel, poor inside, who waves goodbye and then looks ahead. This angel won't need gold-tipped spears like the angels in my night prayer. He just needs some work, a sandwich, and a porch or table where he can sit with someone. I will you a simple angel, a poor angel with whom you may eat a sandwich, be silent, say thanks, and go, both go on your way.

"Do not neglect to show hospitality to strangers, for by doing that some have entertained angels without knowing it." (Hebrews 13:2)

Prison

As a child, I could not imagine life inside a prison. I even hated to see trucks pass our house with cattle locked standing, unable to lie down; chickens jammed into coops, stacked in layers; and turkeys in a shed, crowding each other. I wondered about the feeling and injustice. I read about carloads of prisoners moving toward death camps. In Beatrice, Nebraska, I saw Ben from our church behind bars, alone in a county jail. He could move around and lie down, but could not leave. I bequeath you the feeling of prison.

Father read from the Bible every year reminding us to feed those who are poor, clothe those who are naked, and visit those who are imprisoned. These were not only the words of my father, but of Jesus. It was easy to feel how they needed visiting, but how does a boy get into a prison, and what does he say? I will you the feeling of sometimes being helpless.

Driving past the Nebraska State Penitentiary, I cringed in the back of our '28 Chevy. Guards with guns made sure prisoners did not escape. I felt sick for fright and sick feeling being held prisoner with barbed wire, high walls, and guard-lighted towers. I felt the feeling of being guilty, never able to escape. I met refugees in camps who were held captive, tortured, and escaped. Their stories were full of bravery. They credited God and prayer.

I was sorry that for four weeks Oscar, a horned owl, was in our small basement. He was meant for the sky. But his leg was bruised and, in our house, he was healed. I know a prisoner who was healed while behind bars. I bequeath you praying for the healing of prisoners.

Dietrich Bonhoeffer was one of many who lived in a concentration camp prison. Read his letters, his books, and his prison prayers. In Acts, read the prison story of Peter, and read the letters of Paul written from a prison in Rome.

I once designed a major prison festival in Minneapolis called "Festival of the Lamb." John, a sculptor, found a lamb imprisoned inside a bass wood log. He carved for hours and freed a carved lamb. The lamb was our festival symbol. Prisoners built an altar table, prisoners came to be guests on stage. A man on his deathbed came, for he too was a prisoner. Prisoners sang, clowned, danced, read, worked with clay, told stories. They knew the feelings Paul had while writing letters from prison. I bequeath you the feeling of recovery, freedom, release, being healed. I will you the unlocking of gates that imprison you.

"Peter was kept in prison. . . . Suddenly an angel of the Lord appeared . . . [and] said to him, 'Wrap your cloak around you and follow me.' Peter went out and followed him. . . . After they had passed the first and the second guard, they came before the iron gate leading into the city. It opened for them of its own accord." (Acts 12:5-10)

Broken Heart

Mary did not want to take bread from her father's hand at the communion table. I will you a broken heart at the table of the Lord. She saw a hand with bread broken and the words, "Given for you," and she could not eat; it was the hand of her father.

She was ten, just back from camp. Fido was dead and buried—put to sleep in the past ten days, while she was with eighty other youth at camp in North Dakota. Fido was her dog; they forgot when they decided Fido was a nuisance. Fido was Mary's dog for five years. They had not asked her first. I will you a child's feeling of injustice. I will you hurt and anger of those oppressed who lose their rights.

I was a visitor; we were soon friends. I will you a friend, hurting. You have befriended hurting people. I bequeath you Mary, and Fido. Her eyes were red, her breathing broken, her words forceful: "Tomorrow I will not take holy communion from my father's hand." I will you the honest word of an angry heart: "I will not take the bread from my father's hand." Mary hurt; her dog was dead. They had not asked her.

She wrote me a poem about all this, the night before; her words were few. Mary hurt. I wrote her: "Don't see the hand around the bread, see the broken bread instead, see the broken bread instead." She said she would eat the broken bread if she saw my hand. I will you being beside someone who will eat if you are there. We ate bread broken. We ate together, side by side. I will you someone beside you, broken, eating broken bread with you.

The next week, Mary made her father a gift out of chocolate. I will you a whole broken heart that turns into chocolate. The *Agnus Dei* ends with "give us your peace." That is chocolate.

"Do not let your hearts be troubled. Believe in God,
believe also in me." (John 14:1)

$\mathcal{S}$omeone $\mathcal{F}$amous

He was famous, a historian known to the world; he knew Renaissance. In his later years, we traveled together and staged festivals throughout the country. Often, Dr. Bainton asked me to watch over him as he napped in a hotel corridor, in a corner of a meeting center, wherever he was at his nap time. When it was time, he rested. Then he would briskly raise his head, look me in the eyes, and say: "That's better." I will you the honor of watching over someone older who knows how to rest in a crowd and care for himself.

You know your people of fame who want a few minutes of your care. People wanted to be near Jesus. Can you imagine the feeling of crowds pressing on you? While in a festival, people came from all sides to be close and he felt energy flow from his body. He said the hem of his garment was aflame.

Listen closely to what people of fame say to you. Power can leave as it left Jesus when they touched his garments. Artists show energy bright as light, hot as fire, flowing from a holy person. Under the light and fire was a common man. Dr. Bainton peeled me apples in his cabin, lent me his hand-carved walking stick for walks, recited old poems, showed paintings, read new manuscripts beside a Connecticut fireplace, and confided in tears. He was eighty-four. I will you the friendship of someone renowned, fragile, frail of frame, who gives you slices of apples, walks with you, and phones you in the night.

Now he was alone. Ruth had died. He lived in a simple room with what he needed and no more. A renowned man feasted in a minimal lifestyle. I will you someone great who lives simply and fully.

In the night, he phoned from where he was. If the phone rang at two in the morning, we knew it was Roland Bainton. Lifting the receiver, he spoke these words: "It is I," then a chuckle. "It is I." In the night, I felt not only his name and presence, but tasted the apples and felt the walk and heard the readings. When he said these three words, "It is I," I was half asleep and thought I heard Jesus.

I will you someone who will call you at any hour. When they say, "It is I" you will know who they are, how they feel, what they need, and how they love you. I still hear the voice, "It is I." I will you a Roland Bainton who is famous and needs to talk to you in the middle of the dark. There are such persons near you.

Clown

There are good clowns. They make me new. I also know clowns who make fun of people, kick each other, frighten, hit, and throw fire crackers at each other. I will you a good clown. Many times, I have traveled with good clowns into countries behind the Iron Curtain.

Good clowns have kind feelings. They cry with the sad, but not quite as sad. They are glad with the joyful, but not quite as glad. They are poor with the poor, but not quite as poor. A good clown is a step behind poor and glad and sad, feeling their feelings, and alongside as a caring friend. Being with good clowns is like seeing into a mirror. I will you the countenance of a clown in whom you find yourself and each other.

In Iron Curtain Countries, clowns were not known on main street. We came. Whole towns woke up. Ice cream shops reopened to do trade and feed the clowns. There was handshaking and blessing and smiles between so-called enemies. Clowns dusted benches and sat with people whose guns were set against the west. Good clowns bring enemies together in a single gesture.

Clowns are mostly silent. Their words are felt quietly in the mind and heart. Clown gestures are like scribbles and sketches in the air. Each viewer sees what he or she sees. Together, they create the meaning of the clown routine. I will you the freedom to see what you see and to tell each other. Clowns let each person fill in his or her blank.

I have been with clowns who visit hospitals, sit quietly with dying, hold hands in nursing homes, dance with wheelchair patients, preach, polish shoes, bless, and dry tears. I bequeath you a time with good clowns who are reverent, pray, comfort, adore, and hope. I will you a clown dressed shabbily in a torn shirt, mended pants, and broken shoes, with a tear, and a hope in the heart—a hobo clown with hope. I will you a clown full of laughter—a clown with dance and praise. I will you a clown of wisdom who can figure out, understand, find a path, and lead the way. I will you a clown who leads you to your heart, helps you reflect, stirs a song, begins a prayer, and is still as wind.

In Poland, I saw a clown dust her face with powder as a sign of death. Then came the colors of life, the marks of her special ministry, and finally all the colors and dress of resurrection. All were still as she led us through her transformation. Then she chose her new name. She put on her nose and spoke no more words; her lips were quiet. Every color, motion, mood was now her word. The rest of the sentence was in the eye of the beholder. *Clown* means "clod," "earth," "Adam." I bequeath you to embrace your own creation, and your renewal.

*P*remiere

I will you a premiere. He was guest violinist. The world knew him, and the high school orchestra was honored by his presence. They were ready in black and red uniforms, ready for the violin premiere, a virtuoso in their midst. The baton of Mrs. Pribble came down, the premiere began, and the auditorium was full, expectant, overwhelmed, and proud.

Seven measures and the virtuoso stopped. In the middle of the first page, the violin stopped playing. Mrs. Pribble stopped. All forty-five dressed in red and black stopped. All in the room were silent, worried, waiting, and astonished. The virtuoso had stopped because the violin was not in tune. One string was not in tune. The virtuoso tuned the A string. It only took thirty seconds. The auditorium was hushed, still. Some were embarrassed. What do you say when a virtuoso stops to tune a string?

I will you the nerve to stop when a string is not in tune. Mrs. Pribble's baton began the premiere again. All played to the end. The violin section was in heaven watching, listening, feeling, wanting the music of the virtuoso to fill the room, the world. His music was in their violins borrowed from the school music department. The people heard the A string as never before, and saw it like dancing on a trampoline. Forty-five young teens played their best with the virtuoso.

I will you to play your best when in the presence of a virtuoso, a mentor, a hero, or a beginner. We knew the concert piece from home; our children had practiced. When ended, what would the people do? The virtuoso had stopped the high school orchestra to tune a violin. Mrs. Pribble's baton finished. The music was done. The last note rang through the air, through the walls, and farther. Five hundred people stood, shouted, applauded, and cheered, offering a standing ovation for the school band, and for the virtuoso who stopped in the middle of a premiere to tune one string.

I will you the gift to give a standing ovation, even if a virtuoso, or a beginner, stops to tune an A string in the seventh measure. I will you the meaning of integrity, beauty, trust—these three in the middle of a concert. This I bequeath you: if the string is flat or sharp, fix it, even in public.

"One who walks in integrity will be safe." (Proverbs 28:18)

Lamb

You have heard the words: "The Lord is my shepherd, I shall not want." I do not remember a time when I did not know the twenty-third Psalm by heart, in two languages. I will you a verse in the Bible to love by heart. The picture is clear: the Lord is shepherd, we are sheep. We feel "green pastures" under foot and hear the soft babbling of "still waters." I bequeath you being a sheep to the shepherd where green grass and still waters restore your soul.

I knew sheep in the pasture of Walter Knippelmeyer south of our house. When summer storms came, Walter opened one gate and every sheep hurried under shelter. God is even more a good shepherd than Walter is. In May, I liked the feeling of being a lamb more than a sheep. New born, they danced in the air and circled their mothers leaping, butting, and glad. I will you the feeling of being the lamb of a good shepherd: being safe, having food, hearing a voice you know.

Walter led the sheep; he did not chase them or holler. His voice stayed the same. He was the shepherd. What is your feeling of God's voice? I will you a God who does not chase you or yell, a God who calls, whispers, says your name so you know it is you, walks ahead, stays with you. I will you a God at a table set for you, hosting a feast, or breakfast, more than twelve bales of hay, more than caviar, more than fine wine, and more than green grass.

One April, Walter's mother called me to their kitchen and let me put my hand into a pail of warm milk. An orphaned lamb took my finger and drank the milk; I was a sheep, a ewe, a mother to a lamb. When we sing the *Agnus Dei* in worship, I remember the country kitchen where I learned to be a sheep, a shepherd, a mother, a lamb. I will you being a good shepherd and a good lamb, cared for, known by name, led, fed by God. The word of God is very real.

A Schoolroom

The school I know best had one room. In that schoolroom, all together studied for eight years: Marilyn in grade one, Walter in grade eight, Erhard in grade two, Harold in grade six, Leona in grade five, Gertrude in grade two. I could name them all. Eleven in one room with Loretta our teacher.

I will you a schoolroom you loved: a round stove in the corner, the smell of coal, red hot, kerosene in oiled sawdust aromas on Monday morning. I will you a long chalkboard across the east wall with the alphabet across the top in perfect script, where chalk when erased filled the air with dust. I will you the feeling of old and young kids with a good teacher.

I will you being the only one in grade four and not feeling alone, listening to older ones reciting, helping someone younger learn. I will you large paintings of Abraham Lincoln and George Washington hanging on the south wall, liking them a lot in

February, respectful of the American flag between them. I will you proud feelings when looking at the portraits, believing you are American even though you were only outside of Nebraska five times: once to Jefferson City, and a few times to Minnesota driving through Iowa. I will you a room for learning, where you want to be more than any other place, except outside for handy-handy-over, teeter-totter and softball at recess. What was your most humble place of learning?

Remember the joy of learning at every age—being with a teacher, a mentor, a lecturer, and with persons of every age. I will you the spirit of one room with roll call, where you get to say your own name each day and worry about someone who isn't there. I will you a schoolroom where everything you are learning is on a chalkboard, in a few worn books, under your desktop, in the teacher's mind, or said out loud by someone older or younger. Everyone belonged there, even those who couldn't go on to the next grade. I will you the proud name, "Greenfield School District 62." I will you the fun of tag around a one-room schoolhouse, coloring the hatchet of George Washington's cherry tree, putting your hand up high because you know an answer.

Enjoy learning with others around you who are learning from your answer. People listen to what you say. I will you one room with eleven all learning gladly with one teacher. Jesus met with twelve.

"'Learn from me,' he said, 'for I am gentle and humble in heart, and you will find rest for your souls.'" (Matthew 11:29)

Sights to See

Bless the Lord, O my soul.
O Lord my God, you are very great.
You are clothed with honor and majesty,
wrapped in light as with a garment.
You stretch out the heavens like a tent,
you set the beams of your chambers on the waters,
you make the clouds your chariot,
you ride on the wings of the wind,
you make the winds your messengers,
fire and flame your ministers. (Psalm 104:1-4)

My Heart has felt the wonder of the beauty of the tree,
The bounty of the harvest and God healing by the sea,
The wonder of salvation and the stars inside the sky;
I wonder, wonder why.

My soul has seen the glory of the beauty of the sea,
The diving of the dolphins and the yellow bumblebee,
The waking of the sparrow and its morning melody;
I wonder, wonder why.

My mind does feel the wonder of the rainbow gallery,
The silence of the snowfall and the yellow chickadee,
The whisper of the willow with a mother's melody;
I wonder, wonder why.
Hymn: My Heart
Earth and All Stars
(Augsburg Publishing House)

Roots

Have you seen a prairie root? This week a professor brought prairie grass to a national seminar. The roots were four feet long. He held up new grass for us to see. The roots were four inches long. In Kansas and Nebraska, prairie roots dig deep to find their drink.

So, did the pioneers have long roots? You have read the stories of their months of travel through storms in ships and danger in caravans. They did not forget their homelands and their recipes, and holy days and worship were nurtured by deep roots keeping their strength for generations. Lindsborg, Kansas has traditions with longer roots than found in some villages in Sweden. New Ulm, Minnesota Germans boast the long roots of prairie grass. I will you savoring worthy traditions.

As a child, I believed I was related to Abraham and Sarah, David, Mary and Joseph. I knew them better than I knew my own cousins, aunts, and uncles. When Isaac was to be offered as burnt-offering I cringed and cried. How glad I was each time my cousin Isaac was untied and returned home with his father to mother Sarah. I know more about the travels of Paul in his missionary journeys than I do of the immigration route of my father. God's people have been my family. Their history is in my roots. I bequeath you the roots and legacy of holy writ.

Years ago in Ohio, youth brought a large tree root into the auditorium. We sat in the root at all angles and told old stories. Some were sixty years long, some ten. We were held spellbound in the embrace of a giant elm root. You know how roots nourish. We eat the root of the potato, carrot, turnip, radish, sugar beet. I will you the nurture of the root. I bequeath you an ancient truth, an old hymn, a master work, a proverb, a poem by Tennyson, the sayings of Jesus, a sermon of Paul, a song by Mary. These are our roots. They nurture our minds and hearts. They keep our thoughts from toppling. I will you the strength of what has lived long and is a good root.

Not everything I have lived has taken root yet. It may take root in you. Iris roots need to be separated and replanted. So it is with me and you. There are roots that will bear more fruit when broken apart and given to you. So I give you this legacy of roots. Look below the ground, before your time; see what you have inherited. It is your turn to grow roots that began in other people and places. I bequeath you strength of a prairie root.

"The root of the righteous will never be moved." (Proverbs 12:3)

An Olive Tree

Olive trees do not grow where I live. However, there is one olive tree I know by heart. I saw the tree in the Garden of Gethsemane. There, in the evening light, stood this gnarled tree whose age I could only guess. Some said it was a hundred years old, others said a thousand, some guessed even older. I also would guess older.

Perhaps it was a tree from the time of David. Perhaps the oil of its fruit was poured onto his head and ran down the beard of this anointed king. Perhaps its oil also ran over the beard of King Saul, over the head of the prophet Samuel. This one olive tree at sunset was stunted, strong, bending, bowing and dancing, filled with fruit year after year after year. Its branches were gnarled by heat and drought and winds like hands withered and outstretched to be healed—hands of old men and women I knew at home and saw in Jerusalem.

I will you this strong, gnarled olive tree east of the Jerusalem temple wall.

Sometimes, there is one tree that is all trees, one tree to speak for all trees. This olive tree tells a story for all times. Families came from far lands and bought oil for their lamps from this tree. This tree gave oil to Mary and Joseph on their journey with Jesus. This tree was shade for the disciples one evening after they learned how to pray. This olive tree long ago kept watch over prayer and sleep in its dark garden. This one olive tree gave itself to be cut down and carved into a crèche for a child and into a cross. And the branches of this tree will be carved into new crèches, into shepherds and wise men and mangers and the Christ child.

I will you this tree because its story is yours. It is a story for you; you are part of the story. You will stay with this tree and pray. You will close your eyes to see inside the tree. You will feel the story of the tree, and the olive tree will take you through the gospels. I bequeath you this ancient, gnarled, sturdy olive tree because it is already yours.

"Like the days of a tree shall the days of my people be, and my chosen shall long enjoy the work of their hands." (Isaiah 65:22)

The Other Side

A scout found his way out of woods because he could read the sides of a tree. I bequeath you to know the north side of a tree when you are lost in a forest—the side with moss and mushrooms, the north side, the shady side, the other side from the sun.

Long ago, you learned: there is always another side. I will you the other side of the wall where the enemy fearing our weapons sets missiles facing us. We saw the two sides of the Berlin Wall: one was white, the other had graffiti. It was easy to tell west from east.

I will you the other side of a story when my neighbor shot Rex for killing sheep; my side was the side of a boy who would forgive his own dog for everything. There is the other side for someone condemned to death by a too-white jury. I will you the other side of tracks where mansions are too high to buy, where housing is too cheap to choose, where streetlights are too dim and snowplows come too late.

See the other side. Take a long look. I will you the other side of the embroidery, where a hundred knots and stitches show when thread is tied, when a new stitch begins. What is the other side when people see you? I will you the other side of a rule that warns you and also protects you. The other side of a good law is love.

Our children knew the north side of a tree. If they knew south in a storm, they could find the river, and from there a path home. Wet new moss on elm and ash trees would lead them to the river, then home. I will you the other side of a tree, a hill, a town, a law, a story, a war, pain, fear, and wealth. I will you green moss that shows you where to go. I will you the cry of oppressed; then go and show your mercy. I will you silence after a great noise, a song on the other side of long silence, and a garden after a war. I will you the other side of the elm, the sunny side, the warm side, into which the forest leans to catch its light. I will you the tiny forest tree bent into sunlight, stretching. I will you the child leaning toward someone who knows of light and life, and sees her take her new steps. I will you the north side, the inside, the deep side, the old side, the outside, the other side. I will you the other end of a teeter-totter to play together. I will you the other side of your side. I bequeath you the old saying: "On the other hand."

Hidden Pictures

Leonard hid when I came into the room. I was new in town, a visitor, and Leonard was shy; he did not say much. I was in the room a while. He acted as though he was invisible, sunk deep into a sofa chair, very still. The church people had voted that I should be visitor for a week. Leonard voted "No." His reason, "I don't know him." Leonard was quiet in the corner of the living room—not a word, hardly a breath, not a look, not a word. I will you a Leonard who tries to hide when you come into the room. He asked me not to come.

Leonard did not know me. I knew one more thing about Leonard; I was prepared for the visit. I will you getting ready to meet people who voted for you not to come. "Leonard, I hear you had a butcher shop." That is all I needed to say. Leonard was on his feet, not a word, into the next room, on the floor, under the bed. He crawled out; his hands were full. A box of photos: a hundred old pictures of his butcher shop among Minnesota loggers. Leonard found his world. He knew what to say. He found his voice, his imagination, his inner eyes, his pictures, his stories. One sentence, eight words, freed Leonard. I will you in one sentence to help people say what they see.

Leonard did not stop telling what only Leonard knew best. He was author of this art show, lecturer of a butcher shop, reporter of a logger's festival. At the end of the week, he said to his pastor: "Tell him not to go."

I will you a Leonard who has a festival hidden somewhere, perhaps in a box, perhaps under the bed, in his mind. People of faith ponder.

"The kingdom of heaven is like yeast that a woman took and mixed in with three measures of flour until all of it was leavened."
(Matthew 13:33)

Wind

I love the prairie wind. I watched winter wind bend willows without breaking, dance twigs with ice in sunlight, and whisk one frozen leaf from a limb. I will you the wind: winter wind, the high wind we feel in the tug of the kite string, a wind dancing in a summer sky. I will you the wind that whirled across a field and carried leaves and twigs to another farm, to the horizon, and we wished to follow them there.

You know the ways of the wind; you know how you dream to follow them on a cloud through the sky. I will you the wind that blows across the face in summer and cools us under oak and elm trees. I will you the wind that hums across the southwest corner of a house at night and sings songs in the dark. You know the winds in the dark, swirling outside a safe room. You know winds flapping a flag through the day and rattling shutters at night. I will you the wind you cannot see but makes real what moves inside its embrace. I will you the wind that dried the flood, the wind in the night that showed Nicodemus how to be born again. I will you wind that sweeps dust around a corner and you feel the alley in your face. You have felt the wind that wafts smells of a waterfront, rain in the city, and cut alfalfa in August fields. I will you the wind that shows you something present you cannot see: a factory across town, a bakery two blocks away.

Take the gift of wind. You cannot live without the wind. Inhale it like a prayer. Take it as a gift. I will you the wind you need as living breath to speak your words and laugh your laughter. I will you the wind I was willed, you were willed. Wind is breath, life. I will you the wind.

"You make the clouds your chariot, you ride on the wings of the wind. O LORD, how manifold are your works!" (Psalm 104:3, 24)

A Blind Musician

You must see the fingertips of Holm Vogel, blind from birth, playing Brahms, improvising. You must find Holm Vogel, concert and church organist in Leipzig, town of Johann Bach, now playing the oldest organ in the city.

Do you know a blind musician? Holm has fingertips that see. We crowded into the organ loft and saw him see inside himself and play. Holm began piano at age five, organ at fourteen; he is sixty. He now plays to large audiences around the world. I will you the eyes inside Holm's fingertips as he touches 108 stops of a cathedral organ.

I bequeath you to watch closely. In two minutes, his fingertips find families of organ registers. He whispers Latin names as he touches each register. I will you the touch of a blind person playing a concert to children. They watched him approach the console, find the whole organ, reach with octopus tentacles everywhere, finding every stop and pedal. They were in awe as he discovered the whole organ—outside, inside—with his fingertips. Holm started the organ and told children that the organ breathes. They listened and they believed. Holm Vogel showed the organ's huge lungs, so great a breath that it could play one note all through the night. Holm Vogel showed children sounds of long and short pipes, pipes they could see but only imagine. They believed. His feet played songs as fast as his fingertips. He said pipes are like a family: each different, each important, and all together they are one family of God.

I will you a blind concert organist who helps children see, who wakens a concert organ before their eyes. What will you ask Holm Vogel? Children know what to ask: "Didn't you ever see? How do you learn to play when you can't see? Did children make fun of you? I bet they wouldn't now if they heard you." I will you the gift of children asking. Holm Vogel played fugues, preludes, lullabies, chorales, and folk music. Are you up close with the children?

Children repeated: "How did you learn to do it?" He shows them Braille sheets of music, tells how he memorizes with his fingertips, then finds and memorizes each note on the keys. He feels it in his heart, plays it by heart with his fingertips. Children understand: fingers touching Braille, memorize, by mind, by heart, fingers touching keys. Holm's feet raced over foot pedals. Children clapped at each pause. It was all beautiful, and their eyes did not blink.

A girl closed her eyes all the while to be with Holm Vogel. I will you the sight and fingertips of Holm Vogel, blind from birth. I will you the mind of the girl with eyes closed to be with someone blind. She hears his fingertips with her eyes shut.

Night Time

Nights are as real to me as day. Nights have many parts. They are dark and mysterious, transforming, and full of stars. I know night as I know light. I will you looking into the dawning of darkness, being studious, watching the slow motion of night appearing. You have watched late dusk moving over trees pasted against blue sky, a rising moon, and tired wind. You have seen trees holding still their limbs like giant scarecrows, clouds gliding slowly behind to edge the darkness, and shadows finally sleeping. I will you looking up in darkness, being quiet, standing still as Mars, and eye to eye with old stars.

I will you facing the moon, making a wish, being amazed, whispering a secret in the dark. I will you stars you cannot count, multiplying as your eyes stay on the distance. Say the word *majesty, majesty*. Sing "How Great Thou Art" and "Twinkle, Twinkle, Little Star." I will you the sky in dark rain, in summer midnight, scanning the heavens, your face being washed from above. Face rain in the night, and do what you have never done in dark December.

I ate ice cream in winter, watching a full moon peeking through quilts of clouds. I remember. I will you to do something in a night to remember, being the only one in all the earth facing a frozen December sky somewhere, eating ice cream, blowing bubbles, making a wish, laughing aloud, or whispering the Lord's Prayer. I will you counting stars by twos and fives and tens, running out of numbers, and still counting. I will you seeing galaxies appear, then recounting again when you thought you had counted all. I will you the night sky, where you stay looking until you see what was hidden to you. Lie on earth, face the sky with a song, sing to stars, and sing with stars. I will you night sky above and around, infinite, touching your eyes.

Once in Wisconsin, I lay on a deck with a choir who sang anthems into the night sky. I wish you had been there.

I will you seeing in the dark, knowing a whole night will appear. As a child, I loved the evening song: "O Wie Wohl ist Mir am Abend" (O How Lovely Is the Evening). Night is as real as day.

Stars

I will you a star that centers your soul, saves you.

I found the North Star. I did not know the sky map well, but I knew this one star, and so did she, six thousand miles away on another continent. We had not planned to be apart so soon, so long. I saw the same star seven hours before it shined in her city. The window was just right. I could watch it like candlelight. I toasted the star with wine, made a wish, repeated promises. I talked to a sailor in this distant land. He knew the same star; it saved his life on the high seas. This star was saving my spirit while we were separated. I will you a star that links you across the world.

When little, I watched winter stars through the north bedroom window. At night, these stars took me to places I could never afford and have never seen again. I will you the stars outside windows of childhood, stars that heard wishes, secrets, and stories I never said aloud. I will you stars silent and confident in the sky, through a window you know.

I like stars that dawn in the dark, lights you see as nighttime passes, backstage stars coming forth. I like stars that are faces dawning, thoughts dawning, words dawning, songs dawning in the dark. The dawning of a night star is looking inside myself and finding my own beginning, my own ending. I will you a star that is hidden but not gone, tucked away in the deep inside of night, waiting to dawn.

I will you the star that dawned when squinting my eyes as a child to peek at candles on the altar, the star that dawns when eyes are squeezed with tears or joy or play and you again meet old times, old faces, old places. I will you the star of hope that people of faith once saw and followed to a birth.

In the ancient days of prophets and songwriters, the heavens declared the glory of God. Stars still do.

A Birth

Lois regretted that I was not permitted to be present at the birth of our children. A mother knew this. Nine days after Lois's death, the mother invited me into the birthing room. At 5:20 A.M., the child begins to appear. In fifteen minutes, Nathan was in the arms of his mother. I cut the chord. I played harmonica: "Twinkle, Twinkle, Little Star," and "Little Rock," a song Lois wrote. I had come into the room in time for her to deliver the child. I was grandpa again. Who is this child?

A doctor and nurse were at the mother's feet. The sheets were clean and white; the room was sterile.

My thoughts were in this birthing room and in Bethlehem. Mary was in a cave where animals housed for the night. The aroma of hay, donkeys, sheep, and doves must have been strong. So it was for the "first born of all creation . . . in whom all things hold together." In him and to him all things will hold together and have purpose: hospitals, oxygen tents, stethoscopes, caves, pans of warm water. All things! People, Christians, atheists, rivers, mountains, Moslems, forests, lakes, warriors, hospitals, travelers, children, those who are poor, street people, CEOs, deserts, cities, farms, nomads, merchants, families. Mary did not play harmonica. She sang the Magnificat—a song that reached beyond her hometown into the whole world. Her baby would hold the whole world in his hands. I hear Mary with each birthing breath, repeating a mantra: "Savior . . . Savior . . . Savior."

I bequeath you to honor a birthing time; to be present in person or spirit, wide-eyed, marveling. Mothers and fathers hope and dream at birthing time: who is this one to be, what is she to do, how will he live with war and peace, how will she walk with God?

When I cut the chord of Nathan, I felt responsible. Nathan had been safe in his mother. Now he is on his own, on the outside, with mother and father and us and strangers and friends and foes for a long walk with God. We walk together. It is time for him to be here. It is Nathan's time to be here.

When it was time, you came. When it is time, you will leave. A chord will be cut; you will be in God. There is a right time, not easy, but the right time.

"Mary . . . was expecting a child. . . . The time came for her to deliver her child. And she gave birth to her firstborn son."
(Luke 2:5-7)

Creek

How often I watched an April creek in Nemaha County, Nebraska thawing from a long winter sleep. I wished the world were with me to feel the power and strength of that trickling water. Have you walked a creek with a friend?

I will you a creek in April, waking under ice, breaking through in places so you see and hear a springtime trickle. Follow gurgling water with your friend. See how soon a winter wakes inside an April sun. Break a twig and let water carry it under snow caverns, through white tunnels, out into a tiny open pool, moving south. Follow the twig as though it is a friend, with a name, taking you into a world you want to see.

I will you the joy of naming a twig in a running stream and walking it through thick or thin. Help the twig when stuck behind a weed root so the strength of the trickle will carry it into another white hidden pool, swirling, reappearing downstream by surprise. Follow the April waking water with a friend, and let the twig race you to Mr. Knippelmeyer's fence. I will you the high fence at the south end of the creek that I could not cross. From there, the twig and trickle were on their own. I became a spectator. See swift water run against the forty acres fence, stand there watching the twig pass quickly under barbed wire into a wider stream you may not walk.

I will you being quiet at the fence with a friend, where you let go of a something that was your own. Wave the twig on in silence as it grows smaller and goes farther, moving into the Nemaha River, south and east into a great sea you have never seen. Sail your winter creek into the horizon with your friend and let the winter sun treat you to a voyage of the spirit. You know there is much you will let go. I bequeath you a twig in a running creek. Stand against the fence, still, and see the twig sail safely into a high sea. Let it be a friend, a work, a time, a place. Let it go.

I will you a thawing April creek with a friend and a twig, or two twigs, sailing a journey only you and another know; then let the twig go.

"Send out your bread upon the waters, for after many days you will get it back." (Ecclesiastes 11:1)

An Artist

I followed the life of Melvin from grade three until his death at age seventy-eight. Melvin was my art teacher. He drew. He stayed in the third grade until he turned sixteen. He needed time to draw.

I will you Melvin who, in his last years, drew pigs with a ruler to keep a pig on one page. I met Melvin when I was seven, and sat beside him to see how to draw a cow, a pig, a ship, a chicken, mallards. Melvin showed the strength of a horse when he drew with lead pencil on a lined tablet. I wished to keep each deer Melvin drew. Finally, I drew my own.

I will you a Melvin who knows how to see and draw a deer clearing a high fence. When Melvin drew a horse, I could hear the canter, gallop, trot, and run. I could hear the breath. I could hear ocean waves and feel the swish of wings of ducks rising from a pond. That is what Melvin did best; he drew. I was the only one who took drawing from Melvin. I did it by sitting with him and watching his work. I will you knowing someone who knows what to do well and does it with you. Melvin helped me get dark blue prize ribbons for drawing in county fairs. Melvin was my only art professor.

I will you a teacher who stays in the third grade for five years, and who knows how to draw a pig so you hear the grunt. I met Melvin seventy years ago. The last days of his life, Melvin was still drawing chickens, pigs, pheasant, and horses. In a nursing home, Melvin leaned over notebooks and, with pen and ruler, he measured to fit an entire cow or sheep on one sheet of paper. I will you drawing mallards and deer and oceans to the end. He did not draw missiles and tractors and airplanes and outer space. He did not draw anything made by hand. He drew deer and flowers and willows and snow and rivers and rabbits. Melvin knew nature by heart. He looked inside himself and finally made landscapes with soft lead as his eyes dimmed.

I will you seeing what you can only see inside, landscapes painted from memory. I will you seeing carefully what you will always know by heart. I will you Melvin drawing a lamb he knew when he was little, long ago. I will you seeing an ocean a thousand miles away that you swam in years ago. I will you to see images of joy you once scribbled and remember.

Sparrows

I have long loved sparrows. They are ever present, ever chirping, ever hopping, ever hopeful. A sparrow was near us in India, China, Israel, Russia, Slovakia, Omaha, San Francisco, Marseille, and Berlin. Sparrows are not ashamed of being ordinary in color and habit. The sparrow does not fly away easily. When I was most ill and needed strength, help came from my dear wife and from a daily sparrow at the window. The sparrow knew I was there, and sang as it looked into the north window. I was cheered. I had a visitor who let me be quiet in my rocking chair. You know the miracle of nature, the song, the change of season, the migrations, the coming and going. The sparrow never leaves. I will you the song and presence of a sparrow, or bird of your choice.

A raccoon came to live with us for a season. We raised Scotty from a baby; he knew us, trusted us, and played in our yard. Scotty rode in the bike basket, came on long trips in the car, wrestled, sat at our dining table, and ate a birthday cake mostly unnoticed. Jerry rode down our sled held on our backs and came running before we called his name. It was mysterious to live for a while in the world of a raccoon. Now, years later, a raccoon comes nightly to feed outside my porch sliding door. We do not know each other. He has sat and looked me in the eye for long periods. It is awesome to stare for twenty minutes into the eyes of an animal that lives as "wild" and knows sites and fights and friends we will never know. I bequeath you something "wild" that will stare at you, know you are there, and recognize your caring.

A boa lived with us for years. She went shopping, coiled around our son's waist. Boa, named Noah, was mascot for a rock group and happily clung to the microphone stand making the music sound even better than it was at the Junior High dance. There was no need to fear her. She graced our home. I bequeath you unusual talent of a boa, sparrow, cardinal, chipmunk, raccoon, and crow.

In Iron Curtain days, I knew an old couple who had no children. On a high-rise windowsill, they fed the soft part of the morning bread in bits and pieces to sparrows that always came at seven. They called these sparrows "our children." Their kinship was with birds that had no wall guarding them. Each morning at seven, they fed their "children" who were free to gather. Behind the wall, Fritz and Lisa felt the freedom of the birds. I will you the excitement of God's animals that minister to us. Crows fed Elijah, a great prophet of Israel, and he stayed alive. Sparrows feed me.

Beyond Sight

Hazel had more than twenty-twenty vision. She saw beyond, way beyond, under, around, and through. I will you seeing beyond what is in sight. Her town was not big, a resort village; all people knew each other. Hazel saw more. Hazel knew cities where she had never been, refugee camps she would never walk, strangers across the seas, and hosts of angels. She saw beyond her twenty-twenty vision. I will you seeing beyond what is before your eyes, seeing deeper, beyond.

In a cup of water, Hazel saw milk for a child's thirst. In a dollar bill, she saw a sack of rice for a hungry child. She looked at wheat fields bending at harvest time and saw bags of flour on trucks driving into desert villages. Hazel saw beyond. Some thought she slept while sitting in church. Her eyes were partly shut so she could see a distance beyond normal range. I will you an eyesight beyond normal.

You have looked at one thing and seen more. We all sometimes see way beyond. I was visiting her town. Hazel was at church making quilts, all fabric colors, all textures, sewn with care, tied by hand. Twenty, thirty, fifty, eighty, ninety quilts. I went to the church basement; I saw seven women and Hazel finishing ninety quilts to send off in boxes to people she did not know and had never seen, all strangers. I will you strangers you will not see, yet whom you will love, as did Hazel.

I paid attention to the handiwork of the quilters, and asked to help. Hazel spoke with love: "These are their houses; stitch well." Each quilt was a house to Hazel. That is how she saw beyond. Hazel was a builder of houses. Seven women and Hazel sent ninety houses away in boxes. "Houses" I said to Hazel. "That's what a chasuble is; a little cloth house a minister wears." Hazel was quick to say, "Then we'll make them all ministers." In a moment, Hazel gave strangers cloth houses and made them ministers. We waved to the bus, leaving the little town, on the way to a desert of refugees.

I will you the eyes of Hazel to give strangers ninety homemade houses, chasubles. Keep looking, farther, deeper, closer; there is more.

"Lift up your eyes all around and see." (Isaiah 49:18)

Shadows

Our family watched a walnut tree grow from seed next-door to the west. Day and night, it now casts great shadows into my yard. I will you the shadow of Kenny's walnut tree through the yard in full moon. I will you winter morning shadows, when earth is white and sun outlines trees on snow. Watch them move like still life across landscape and see time reach in all directions.

You played with your shadow as a child. Take time to watch shadows. See shadows follow you when you walk into light. Look back at shadows, play as though you're leaving a place you like, then looking back to stay a little longer. I will you shadows that make giant trees seem small, or make your shadow too little to find in their shade. See light and dark play. Find someone who will still love a shadow with you.

I will you shadows of a full moon when trees from another yard lie across your house and picnic table like a black and white painting over you. For a few hours follow night patterns from next-door, borrow your neighbor's willow tree, apple tree, or chimney in the night. I will you shadows that climb a wall you walk by; mime your walk, every move. See your walk against a high wall in the dark. Play with shadows. Find them for the first time, and see them disappear. Watch for shadows on a trip.

I will you the shadow of clouds moving slowly through bright sky on a warm day. In shadows, you will stay cool. Watch days partly overcast. I will you patches of shadows you see from above, from a tall building, when on a mountaintop, from forty thousand feet. Stay in a shadow and pray, with your eye on the shadow.

I will you the shadow of a walnut tree across the front yard in December, and the shade of a midnight cloud moving past a quarter moon. I will you the quiet of a shadow that rests without moving, and dances slowly if the wind blows far above. I will you the shadow of a squirrel running into its shadow with the sun behind, of a bird moving above its shadow on a lake. See the shade and the sun together. I will you dark and light, bright moonlight and deep patterns painted around you. I will you the joy of hiding "in the shadow of [God's] wings" (Psalm 63:7).

Running

More and more, I am keeping my eye on children, as years go by. We are playing more, as an older person can play. In the 1970s, we had house church; thirty people met each week to worship in someone's home. This Sunday, it was Dana's home. A nine-year-old waited at the curb with the greeting: "Herb, draw a name. This will be your partner for thirty minutes in the yard." I drew the name Eric, age two. What would I do with a two-year-old for thirty minutes outside in the yard? Eric would decide. He looked at me, grinned, and ran through the grass, stopped, bent over, stared and shouted, "See." I looked; it was a little stone. He handed me the stone, a gift. It was Easter. What did Eric, age two, know about the Easter stone rolled away? Eric ran again, through the grass, laughing. I followed, running.

When have you last run with a child? Do you know the feeling of being led this way? I believe you have this spirit, so I bequeath you Eric. A child knows where to run and when to stop. Do you know? Eric ran, and stopped; he bent over, stared, and shouted, "See." I looked again. He found a yellow dandelion and picked it; the flower was mine, a flower on Easter day. What did Eric know about the Easter lilies in chancels of churches? I knew about Easter. Eric knew about flowers. Have you run with two-year-olds?

"See!" What a wonderful word for a bulletin cover. Eric was running, and I was following. He began to tumble in the grass. I heard the message: "See Eric." He stood and raised his hands into the air. I was to see him, pick him up, hold him in the air, and on my shoulders. I lifted Eric because that is what he wanted to do with me. Eric was leading me in this Easter Introit and he was not finished. "See! See!" He shouted, and pointed to the people in the house. All were to see Eric and Herb on Easter, together.

Much later, I raised my hands to God and whispered, "See." Eric had been leading us toward God in an Easter liturgy. I bequeath you an Eric and all little ones to lead you as God says children will.

"A little child shall lead them." (Isaiah 11:6)

A Good Word

"The LORD is my rock, my fortress, and my deliverer,
my God, my rock in whom I take refuge,
my shield, and the horn of my salvation, my stronghold."
(Psalm 18:2)

There is a Rock that follows where we travel,
We stop to rest; the Rock is by our side.
We hear the wind, the storm, the dark, the danger,
There is a cleft, inside the Rock we hide.
Christ is the Rock, our anchor in the journey,
The mountain height, our silent resting place;
Christ is the Rock, deep fountain in the desert,
The healer of all thirst, our drink of grace.
Hymn: Christ, Be My Rock

Thanks

Thanks is a right word for most everything that happens. When Lois died, I begged God for what I could not have. It was hard to sleep. I remembered something I read forty years ago in a workshop. Give thanks first; then ask and intercede. The thank-you list grew long. She left so much for which to thank. With giving thanks, I felt a deep reverence and gratitude. I learned to say thanks for what I have when sadness comes, is happening, or is long over. I will you saying thanks for what you did not thank. Give thanks for what you inherited, what blesses you and is now in you.

I keep thanking Mrs. Buchholz. Reverence was her lifestyle. She taught me reverence when I was seven. She tiptoed to her son's grave, looked down, standing in awe. I saw her reverence as I felt reverence in Sunday worship. I saw her bow over the grave, pull tiny new weeds, water flowers in bloom. I saw her read the engraved stone again and believe. I will you those who taught you reverence, whom you did not yet thank.

After sixty years, I gave thanks to Mrs. Buchholz. I read the letter aloud on the cemetery. Her children's children listened. "Dear Mrs. Buchholz. Thank you for teaching me reverence when I was seven. I watched you, for I mowed the cemetery. Seeing you, I practiced awe and holiness. Thank you for teaching me. Two years later, I needed to do it myself with my family. I did not thank you then for I was nine. You died eighteen years ago; I am writing you to thank you, Mrs. Buchholz, because it is not too late. Thank you." I will you the word *thanks*. It is never too late to thank Mrs. Buchholz.

"P.S. Mrs. Buchholz, What you taught me about reverence when I was seven helped me when I was 77, when Lois died." I am saying thank you a lot.

"O give thanks to the LORD, for he is good;
for his steadfast love endures for ever." (Psalm 106:1)

Humble

Prophets were not always popular. Some were persecuted; some had bounty on their heads. They commented on war, peace, justice, wealth, taxes, poverty, politics in the name of the Lord. They bowed before God.

Who are the prophets today? Who are prophets in the church? Do we want them in the pulpit? Do we have them in congress? Are they our community leaders? Are they songwriters and poets? Are prophets foreign correspondents? Are prophets late-night hosts in comedian clothing? Do they know when to bow before God?

Micah speaks a prophetic word. "What does the LORD require of you but to do justice, and to love kindness, and to walk humbly with your God?" (6:8). This could be a church's mission statement: do justice, love kindness, walk humbly. How does this translate in our workplaces, playgrounds, parishes, homes? How do I do justice? How do I love kindness? How do I "love to do" kindness? Micah is calling for a change of heart, to bow humbly before God.

Micah's words are like the attitudes of Jesus. Love is about attitudes.

How do we "walk humbly with God"? This is a journey we all walk, the walk with God. God gives us the way, a lamp for the feet, a light for the path, the walk. God shows the way behind us and before us and in us. The whole way. It is God's way. We do not make up the path. We walk humbly before God.

What makes me humble in this walk? This is more than a walk with each other, with family, members of the parish, neighbors, a nation. I am walking with God. With God! God gives me this right, this life, this walk.

I look out my window and see remaining autumn leaves. All life is God's life, changing, growing from season to season. I see myself at this age in the mirror and I see a picture on the dresser when I am nine. I see life changing, growing. Who gave me all these years? Who gave me dawn and dusk 25 times, 250 times, and more?

I bequeath you this humble walk.

Prepositions

Until, By, Into, After, From, Across, Against, With,
Toward, On, Among, Around, Along, Of, To

I will you prepositions. Prepositions have long fascinated me. In country school I liked seeing them on the chalkboard and then using them to make sentences more playful. Prepositions also were part of my real world. I could climb *into* a tree, slide *down* a culvert and jump *across* the creek. Much of my life I have been *among* people and felt how visible and invisible *among* can feel. As a husband and father, I could use all the prepositions as I stood *for* and *against* things, went *with* the family *on* long trips, and often stayed up *until* midnight waiting *for* teenagers to come home. I will you all prepositions and the ones you know best.

Through the years, I have studied the Bible, watching prepositions move the words of Paul's long sentences into deep meanings. I felt prepositions in Bible readings during Lent, in stories of Christ's suffering and death. I have watched prepositions in hymns and prayers to find the flow of authors' feelings. These are the same prepositions that make us feel the morning news, help us understand our e-mails and our phone calls.

Congregations hired me to teach communication skills to teachers and councils. Often, we sat near playgrounds and watched children play. We looked at them enjoying the spaces and movements of prepositions: *for, against, into, after, over, under, between, among, inside, through.* We marveled at how children played prepositions without being able to spell or label the words. Then we saw how, as adults, we still play out prepositions in our behavior at meetings, around tables, in daily life. We marveled at the power of simple words in speech and in action.

I will you the joy of prepositions you have known since your birth—the spaces and movements God gives us to play out feelings and thoughts, the words God gives us to express those feelings and thoughts. You know the power of words and their meanings. You are a thoughtful person who cares how you move *through* life *among*, *with*, and *for* others. Therefore, I will your father the enjoyment of prepositions, especially those that make for peace. Jesus said, "I am with you always." *With* keeps us close.

$\mathcal{H}$onor

An early picture of honor for me was my father tipping his hat in Daykin, Nebraska, a town one block long. Father tipped his hat, for he knew them all. He tipped his hat to women and older people. "Honor you father and mother"; I learned the command in two languages, and by practice. I did not tip my hat; I stood when the Heckels or Mrs. B. F. Henry came into the house. We stood when the ministers and wives came to visit. We stood and hoped they would soon sit so we could. Honor was something we had to do with our whole body. Honor comes in many postures. I will you the deep rich feeling of honor.

I like honoring the flag in school, especially country school. We went outside into the wind and felt the air and distance of America. The furthest we'd ever been was Omaha, or Jefferson City, or Radio City Music Hall by way of the radio. I could feel all of America at the flagpole. It was the same feeling I had when looking at the painting of Jesus in church and President Roosevelt in the bank calendar. Honor was like standing in front of the Heckels, my brother's godparents. I bequeath you the high calling of honor. You know the anchored, tall feeling when standing to honor.

Farmers knew when to stop shocking grain and plowing and even threshing to stand with their straw hats over their breast, facing a hearse going by on the country road. They were silent as they were in a world war when taps were blown. I bequeath you the reverence felt inside honor.

First on radio and then later in person, I heard honor in applause. The sound of clapping and cheering, shouting "Encore," and people on their feet stomping for one more song.

Honor is sometimes felt with the whole body, out loud, and will not quit until satisfied. Honor can be done in absolute silence, hardly breathing, as before the tomb of the Unknown Soldier or an anthem that needs silence to linger and stay in the heart. I will you great moments of honor, when you honored and were honored.

A mother after delivery must have a look of honor as she holds the newborn. Who has not honored an infant? They have come from the world we will again reenter. They know a long silent world we have forgotten. They are in touch with their inner needs. They are vulnerable and will require honor and care to live. I will you honoring what is needful: a broken wing, a broken branch, a broken life. I will you the gift of standing to respect what is worthy; I will you the gift of honor, and of knowing when to be silent, to bow, or tip your hat.

"Outdo one another in showing honor." (Romans 12:10)

Patriotism

Patriotism grew early in me. It happened in grade three as I stood in our country school and saluted the flag. It was not the flag as much as the words "to the United States of America." I knew what it meant to belong to Nebraska and Nemaha County, but now I could belong to all the states in America, and they belonged to me. By keeping my eyes on the flag, I could let the words fill up inside me the way I felt full when reciting a whole poem without a mistake in front of people. I was proud to belong to something so big.

When were you first patriotic? What filled you with pride? George Washington and Abraham Lincoln hung on the south wall, side by side. One couldn't tell a lie; the other wanted all people to be free. I was proud to belong to these two men who were looking at me from the paintings. Since they were near the chalkboard, I memorized their faces the way I knew the picture of Jesus over our piano at home. The only other president I knew was Franklin Roosevelt, but he was not hanging in our schoolroom. He was in Washington, D. C. Washington and Lincoln were always in the room, they stayed there all night and over the weekend. So I was loyal to them and to the flag that stayed beside them.

Patriotism had little to do with war and politics and government. Mine had to do with standing with all the children and teacher and making a pledge with my right hand over my heart. That was like taking an oath or saying, "cross my heart and hope to die." Harold and Leanna and Erhard and the others saw and heard me doing it; so I was accountable. That is a feeling I felt. I was standing and making a choice. It was like voting when you really weren't old enough.

Do you recall your childhood feelings about saluting the flag and being American? My father was an immigrant and so I thought of two countries while being patriotic. I heard the other land might become our enemy some day. I was so full of being an American that I knew they would not be my enemy. I could keep that from happening with this feeling inside me. If we all quit telling lies and all wanted freedom the way Washington and Lincoln wanted (I could see it in their eyes), then all we needed to do was put our right hand over our heart and say, "liberty and justice for all." While still standing, we'd sing "God bless America, land that I love," the way Kate Smith did on radio. I will you the innocence and power of a child's patriotism.

Ubiquity

Ubiquity *is a word easier to describe than define.*

Louie made birdhouses with crosses so birds could come home to God. Louie saw more than meets the eye. He looked beyond what he saw. Louie looked at a tiny stone until he saw its mountain. Louie saw something close up until he stood inside its universe. Louie could look at a twig and see a forest. I will you Louie's perspective.

I will you looking at one star and seeing galaxies. You have watched the sky unfold stars in the dark. You have studied a single bloom until you saw petals, stamen, and the markings in the leaves. I will you finding a single desert blossom and seeing in it a colored landscape, or a distant horizon. I will you watching a butterfly close up and seeing a Picasso in the art gallery.

Louie saw a lot more than eyes can see. He looked inside and through and beyond. He studied birds in flight. They belonged to his birdhouse with a cross. Press your ears toward the song of one Canada goose and hear a hundred honking their way in a thousand-mile skyway. I will you Louie who looks close and sees far and hears more. In church, he sees a meal in a little wafer. He sees wheat and rain and sun and wind and harvest in a piece of whole wheat toast.

I will you a close look at a twig until you see the branch, the trunk, and the root. Look down on the tips of buds and see apples that will hang there. I will you eyes of Louie, who in the middle ages would be professor of ubiquity. I will you seeing a feast in a broken wafer, and all thirst quenched in one cup of wine. Wave to one bird in flight and join it to the end. I will sometimes being like Louie, looking deep, seeing near and far off at once. I will you Louie, who sees one drop of rain and sees God.

"If I ascend to heaven, you are there; if I make my bed in Sheol, you are there. If I take the wings of the morning and settle at the farthest limits of the sea, even there your hand shall lead me, and your right hand shall hold me fast." (Psalm 139:8-10)

Trust

Love was a household word in our home. We sometimes spoke it as *trust*. Love is a trait of good mothers. My father repeated the words of the Lord about trust; trust had also to do with faith. Trust was holy, whether cited in scripture or shown in the harvest field by a farmer. In graduate school, I learned that I. Q. could be raised in children by rocking them, through love, by building trust. I will you the gift of trust, which can grow faith, intellect, love.

You need trust as an infant or as an adult. In country church school, father showed me trust recorded in the Bible. I learned proof that God can be trusted being with my mother, who taught trust in her cooking and care. Mother was proof that God can be trusted. She repeated trust in many ways. Father taught me that God can be trusted; mother proved it. Perhaps it was the same with you.

Father taught that God created "everything after its own kind." This means cows beget calves and sheep beget lambs. This verse was most real when bananas shipped from Central America arrived in our kitchen. Mother sorted through the banana bunch to make sure no Black Widow spider was hiding to harm us. Hunting that spider was a dangerous event in our country life; this was a moment of great trust. We trusted mother; if there was a spider lurking in the bunch, mother would find it. We trusted her protection in the kitchen. We trusted father in the Bible. That picture has stayed with me. I bequeath you childhood times when trust was close and clear from both kitchen and scripture.

Seventy years later, I wrote a hymn of trust. "Bananas bear bananas, and apples bear their fruit; the vine begets the vineyard and branches have their root." Nature and the Bible agree. Bees beget bees; apples bear apples. God is a dependable. God abides by laws. The greatest law is this: "God's mercy endures forever." Creation has rules; salvation has rules. So the hymn continues: "Good Friday looks for Easter, and graves will open wide; the hill, the cross, the glory, and then the other side."

In a recent trust hymn I wrote, "Praise, praise to God, we give you thanks. You formed the deep and distant past, all tiny moments yet to be; you gave the vision that will last. You made the resurrection law; you founded one eternity." I like the thought of a "Resurrection law," born of God's love. We trust the law of gravity in creation. I will you to trust the law of love. I will you to trust forgiveness and resurrection. The strongest law is not the law of gravity but the law of love.

Credo: "I believe in the forgiveness of sins,
the resurrection of the body and the life everlasting."

Apology

It is not too late to ask. Did I hear what you asked me? Did I listen to your feelings when I was told again and again? Was I too busy when you invited me to come to something you were doing? I ask for your forgiveness. I know I still owe apologies.

I will you the fact that it is not too late to apologize. What do you need to ask?

Did I care when your homework was too much? Was I too busy when you were being sick, being glad, being back home on vacation? Did I travel too much and you missed me? Did I feel a loss you felt? Did I walk too fast, turn away, cut you off? Was I sick when you wanted me to be well? Did I miss concerts you wanted me to attend? Did I yell and frighten you?

It is not too late to ask. I will you the desire to apologize, though it may seem too late. Apologize in prayers, on a walk, by phone, in writing. Talk face to face. Review times you were too hurried, unsympathetic, preoccupied. There were plans never finished. Were we a burden? Did we make someone cry?

I will you the grace to apologize for what you did not do or say. I will you the love to say "I'm sorry," even now.

I will you the gift of hearing an apology you were not ready to hear. When possible, I go to worship early. I review words and deeds said long ago, and those still to be done and said. Apologizing comes in many words and actions. Some very real apologies are never said aloud.

"I'm sorry" is a biblical way of life.

"Be kind to one another, tender-hearted, forgiving one another, as God in Christ has forgiven you." (Ephesians 4:32)

Love

Love is a little word with a big heart.

You were born . . . for God's steadfast love endures forever. A much-needed rain began at midnight . . . for God's steadfast love endures forever. We woke at seven and felt rested . . . for God's steadfast love endures forever. God spread out the earth upon the waters . . . for God's steadfast love endures forever. The flowers in our garden are in full bloom . . . for God's steadfast love endures forever. Nathan was born at 5:22 A.M. . . . for God's steadfast love endures forever. Roger is expected to make a full recovery . . . for God's steadfast love endures forever. The angel of the Lord said, "Behold I bring you tidings of great joy!" . . . for God's steadfast love endures forever. Jesus was thirty-three and he said: "Into your hands I commit my spirit." . . . for God's steadfast love endures forever. Jubilation choir sang "All is calm, all is bright" . . . for God's steadfast love endures forever. You are alive . . . for God's steadfast love endures forever.

Steadfast love . . . forever. Steadfast love . . . forever. Just think!

In Psalm 118, Israel recorded their nation's history as song, with the refrain after each sentence: "for God's steadfast love endures forever." Imagine telling the story of each week, this day, our family, pausing after every sentence while all sing: "for God's steadfast love endures forever."

Lois cherished a butter plate that she often brought to church to show children. Around the rim was written: "Love, love, love, love, love." With this plate, we taught many children the meaning of Holy Communion. Bread on this plate said it all. I cannot find the plate. I picture it and am reassured that God is about love. Picture your life with these words interspersed: "Love . . . love . . . love . . . love."

Once God's steadfast love was newborn, in a cave, in a tiny town, beside a healing pool, on a hill on a tree, in a garden tomb. Now where is this love of God? Here! Here! Here, in every tiny nook and cranny, in every hut and mud house and cave and castle, in every hovel and hospital room, in every trench and tank, in every mass grave, in every raging sea, in every place on earth, in the water, in the air, in space, in you.

I bequeath you believing that God has filled earth with love, that love permeates the universe, all the time, everywhere, for all.

"The earth is full of the steadfast love of the LORD." (Psalm 33:5)

Connected

Gladys was in communion when she woke, slept, drank her tea, phoned. Like old Hannah, her lips were always moving with the Spirit; we could not always see them. Gladys's whole life was being in relationship. She looked up a lot. We are always under God. I will you a continual life of communion.

Gladys said, "Child of God" in the middle of everything, seldom out loud. She practiced connecting life with God. Gladys grew old, slept much, dreamed. She sang songs in the dark. Gladys slept inside the family of God. She was never alone. I bequeath you being connected to everything, everyone, the One.

She crossed everything with a sign of holiness, with her fingers, eyes, and thoughts. I will you this connection, awake or sleeping. God was not a subject to her. God was more constant than air and breath and light. God was older and newer, darker and brighter, slower and faster than anything Gladys knew. Gladys could take people to God through a story of shoes or a play based on a hat or a well-prepared prayer. Her Bible was marked and frayed; she filled margins with scribbling. What was once on stone and in parchment was in Gladys's spirit and songs. I will you God's word in your imagination. Gladys prayed for others; if there was still time she told God about herself.

I will you being connected continually to family, neighbor, stranger, enemy, saints, the universe. Gladys talked with God when others talked about God. Gladys was in prayer while she spoke words of prayer; petitions for others always came first. When she sat at table she sat upright as though before a queen or king. She was in the presence of majesty; surrounded by the whole household of God. She looked through breakfast and every meal straight into heaven, and remembered all who were hungry and poor. I will you the life of Gladys who believed that God's will in heaven was God's will on earth. When she sat at our table it was as though St. Francis of Assisi was our guest.

I will you feeling the spirit that whispers "Thanks" in the middle of a sunrise, "Lord, have mercy" in the middle of the five o'clock news, and "Care for the poor," when supper is served. I will you a spirit connected to God and to all of the creatures God so loves in the world.

Swivel

Emma swiveled. Emma was a whole person. She felt being Emma from head to foot, way inside and all around. She looked in all directions and was a truly present woman. I will you Emma and her art of looking back, taking, remembering, reminiscing, and reflection. I will you all who, like Emma, keep something dear from the past alive, not throwing away something before they know its story.

We have kept an orange until it is hard and small as a yellow golf ball to give as a keepsake. We saved a favorite sapling that died too soon and will be a walking stick. We saved writings and drawings of when you were little, and knowing when you are older that you were that girl or boy, and still are. I will you the good feelings I have of my drawing strong deer and Joe Louis and ships on high seas when I was nine and wanted to be safe and strong. I will you keeping a worn shoe that took you through many places of life.

In all this I bequeath you an Emma when you meet her. Look in all directions and see what is still worthy.

Give a worn shoe an intentional future. Paint it, plant in it a flower, give it to someone young who wants your story and loves you. Bury it under a rose bush for its future. I will you what is not over. Keep tasting good things. Remember the aroma of wilted lilacs. I will you the thought of an old bed on which mothers and fathers loved. I will you a story a mother told you on her lap, feeling God near as she read, believing her eyes and voice.

I will you what is behind you, past, and not over. Choose it, hold it like fine porcelain, and set it where others can ask: "What is it to you?" Emma stood in our house church and pivoted, saying, "You is lookin' at de lady of de Lawd." She swiveled as she spoke, saying, "You got to look where you was to see where you's goin'." I will you places where "ya was" and where you "is goin'." I will you the art of Emma, looking back and forth, around, inside, remembering how you got here. Sometimes swivel.

In a vision of "whirling wheels," with "eyes round about"

turning in all directions, Ezekiel saw cherubim with the "semblance of human hands under their wings," and above them "the glory of the Lord" (Ezekiel 10:8-18).

$\mathcal{M}$mmm

I will you *Mmmm*. Betty licked bowls in her mother's kitchen and learned the word *Mmmm* with chocolate. She was not very old but she was very ill. In the height of her career, she was now at the end of life. She was ready. I will you to be ready even if death seems to come too early.

In her mother's kitchen, Betty learned *Mmmm*, a word good to the very end. I came to visit her; this was the last time. We did not know what to say. Betty did not seem to think it was the end. She was still licking her mother's kitchen bowl. Her mind was full of earthly graces; she still smelled the aroma of the cake in her mother's oven. Betty spoke of her mother; this was her medicine.

You know this kind of visit, the last one. There is a Betty in your life. I bequeath you this gift of saying goodbye.

I was leaving and Betty asked me to say something: a few words, not many, something important. She had told me of the soft quilt her mother had made for her forty years before: blue, white, pink, and lavender. I thought of four things to say that Betty knew; not many words, and important.

I will you four things to know and say at the end. I covered Betty with her mother's quilt four times. My words were short: "I believe in God." Betty hummed "Mmmm." "I believe in resurrection." Betty whispered "Mmmm." "I believe in life everlasting." She said "Mmmm." I said "Amen." She hummed "Mmmm" for the bowl she licked with mother, and the quilt she knew was pink and blue forty years before. "Mmmm" was her last word.

I will you a truly delicious, comforting last word: *Mmmm*. Betty meant to say *Yes* and *Amen* and *Verily*. Are Jesus' last words: "Into Thy hands I commend my spirit" the same as "Mmmm"?

Alright

While I was writing this book, our family buried my wife Lois, their mother and grandmother. We waited a year before going back, so the grandchildren would grow and could hopefully remember the celebration. On what was once a shepherd's field, we walked toward the site under black umbrellas white with soft falling December snow.

Children from ages one to seven peered into the silver vault as did disciples into the grave of Jesus. They were curious and prepared to do something very special. I will you curious children at a gravesite. One held a scroll on which she had written and drawn a message. They lifted the lid of the urn holding the ashes. The urn had been made by one of their fathers when he was twelve. They each placed a Mum blossom into the vault. With an aunt, they had made a quilt using scraps of grandmother's sewing. The quilt was wrapped around the urn to make it pretty and keep it warm in the winter. Another special cloth from her sewing box was wrapped around the urn to make sure it would stay warm. It was much like tucking in a doll. I bequeath you children at a gravesite.

We held hands in the cold and sang a child's song grandma had written many years ago. We prayed. I pointed to the words and names that will be on the tomb plaque. There were the words of the song we had sung: "Love, love, love; that's what it's all about." There was the name Lois. My name was printed beside it, but not the day I would die, and the words, "Earth and all stars, sing to the Lord a new song." None of them was in a hurry to leave. The youngest stood alone, pondering, as though he had just come from where Lois went.

We blessed the grave, grandma, and each other, and we believed in the resurrection. I bequeath you sometimes letting children guide you through tears. As we turned to go an uncle asked the three year old: "Are you afraid to die?" She answered quickly: "Oh, no, it will be alright." A little later he asked her the same question. Again she promised: "Oh, no, it will be alright." That is what I will you at the grave of a loved one. It will be *alright*.

A Right Spirit

"Create in me a clean heart, O God, and put a new and right spirit within me. Do not cast me away from your presence, and do not take your holy spirit from me. Restore to me the joy of your salvation, and sustain in me a willing spirit." (Psalm 51:10-12)

"The fruit of the Spirit is love, joy, peace, patience, kindness, generosity, faithfulness, gentleness, and self-control. There is no law against such things." (Galatians 5:22-23)

Music is the voice of heaven,
Instruments to quiet fear,
Melodies of Holy Spirit
Humming dry a hidden tear;
Music is the voice of heaven,
Seraphim sing through all spheres.
Hymn: Music Is the Voice of Heaven

I will you the winter, the summer, the spring,
The mountains that whisper, the angels that sing;
I will you the rain and the seed in the ground,
The grain and the bread when the harvests abound.

I will you sweet comfort, the sleep in the night,
The medicine hid in the source of all light;
I will you the life where new miracles hide,
The secrets of healing with blessings inside.

I will you the Spirit of worlds still unseen,
Of caring, of sharing, and places between,
The Spirit of God hid deep in all space,
The Spirit of glory, the Spirit of grace.
Hymn: I Will You

Questions

Years ago, students were surprised when I assigned them to write ten thousand questions. They were more surprised when they found they were able to do it. An inquisitive spirit grew in them. These were not only questions with "true" or "false" answers. As the lists grew, there came questions for wonder, awe, and an open spirit. Their eyes opened as they asked the color of grace, the sound of trust, the season of hope, the texture of faith. Most made connections and formed meanings they had never before considered. Perhaps earlier, in their years of play and scribbling, they played with questions of shadows and wind and falling leaves and clouds. But as the years passed, such questions had faded.

I will you an inquisitive spirit that asks questions for which you do not expect an answer. Because you are curious, you will consider this bequest. Your life will widen and deepen with an inquisitive mind. And it will focus, center. In the middle of a cluster of a hundred questions is the main question. I will you the main question, the bottom line, the heart of curiosity.

I will you prayers that ask the questions of children: *How? How? How? Why? Why? Why?* In prayer, the answer is often in the good question. When we ask God the right question, we already have the answer. When you ask a friend the right questions, you will know the friend.

How do you practice asking? Ask a tree ten questions. Most of these will be good to ask a close friend: *How are you? How did you get here? Who notices you? Who cares for you? What is your favorite season? What happens when you are in need?*

Think back to your childhood. How did you talk to your teddy bears and childhood friends? Were your questions sometimes more about feelings and relationships than getting right answers? I will you questions of the heart, full of feeling. I will you questions of color and seasons and moods. I will you questions of faith and love and trust. I will you questions of peace and compassion. I will you some of the ten thousand questions students asked forty years ago. Their questions are still stored in blue tubs in my garage, in me, and in them. I bequeath you the right questions that lead you to the good answer.

The Owl

Oscar, a horned owl, flies the Minnesota valley forever. I will you the sight and sound of Oscar, whom we came to know. Our children brought the horned owl wrapped in a winter jacket to our house. The way the owl was wrapped and placed in our warm basement, we felt the story of swaddling clothes and a manger. It was Christmas time; the thought was easy.

I will you a wounded owl being cared for, a harmed creature in need. Trappers had left an owl with his leg wounded, infected, and he was starving. Our veterinarian felt honored to treat a grown horned owl. Immediately, the name became, officially, Oscar. The neighborhood knew. Oscar took on our family name: Oscar Brokering. I will you a wounded bird as member of your family. Oscar healed in the basement. He perched inside a screen cage, fasted, rested, stretched, and often exercised the length of the basement. We learned to be together. He was fed with caution. His feather size increased when Mechant the cat came near. Oscar learned to know us.

I will you a horned owl that learns to know your presence, trusts you, and eats from your hand. It was an honor to be accepted by Oscar. He was a dignitary. He had flown to heights we could not ascend. He knew night places by heart. Oscar could travel more than sixty-miles-an-hour within seconds. I will you the magnificence of a creature called "wild" that recognizes you. Oscar healed slowly, flew the basement length one more time, and, before we were ready to release him, found the sky. We feared he was not ready to be on his own. Once he was in the air, he did not return. The doctor said Oscar would make it.

I will you to worry about the safety of something wounded, freed after being captive. We still look up and expect to see Oscar soaring. The surprise we brought home wrapped in a worn cloth jacket was now in the sky, out of sight. But Oscar is not gone. We see an owl; we say Oscar. I will you the presence of something you love when you cannot see it. I will you Oscar who does not quit the sky, sings melancholy tunes in the dark, and knows you.

Oscar came to us forty years ago. Last night I heard an owl. Oscar is back. He is decorating the night this Christmas. May a sound long past decorate your day.

*S*nowman

Making a snowman can feel like being God. Giving the snowman a hat and a carrot, mud mouth and coal eyes is like feeling what God must have felt making Adam from mud. Those were my child thoughts. I will you a snowman made by your hands.

Through the years, whether a snowman, woman, child, or clown, I have wanted to breathe into it the breath of life. Do you remember a snowman you rolled and patted and dressed and gave a face? I will you something you make by hand as big as yourself, or bigger, and saying: "It is very good." Stand beside it, feel you have a friend made by your own hand, and your own imagination.

I will you making something life-size that feels lifelike. Have a child with you, and give your creation a hat, a tie, a carrot nose, a jacket, glasses, shoes and gloves, a scarf, a book, a bowl of cereal. Give it what you want it to have. Make yourself a winter friend. I will you a handmade friend. Feel yourself God-like, shaping a new person, giving something character, making sure it will stand up, putting it where you and others can see, and making it a story to tell. Look at it from all sides so it's real all the way around, like a Roman sculpture. Make the face like your own. Give it eyes to see, and ears that hear.

I will you making a snowman that has feelings, spirit, moods, and emotions. Give your snowman an attitude you like. Pretend you breathed and it came alive, and it does what it wants. Can you make it a story for someone who needs to see what you have made? Together, give it a name.

I will you the desire to be creative, to make something great with your own hands, to make something after your own likeness. It may not be out of snow but of wood and paints and a recipe and dough and cloth and thread. Make it alone, or with someone you know well. Tell each other what you are making, the feelings, and the reason. I will that you make something of snow or paints or wood or flowers that connects you with something human in the world, inside yourself. I will you making something of your own and feeling Godlike.

Cry

Sometimes cry. I bequeath you the gift of sometimes crying. I cried last night. For the second time in twenty years, I saw the film *A River Runs through It*. See a film and cry. Read a poem and cry. The film helped me cry as a young boy, a brother, a preacher, son of a preacher, a husband, father, and old man. Sometimes cry for all kinds of reasons that go way back, way inside, or way ahead. I cry for times I will never see on earth, lives grandchildren will live that I will never know. I have cried for times my mother and father did not tell us about. I can feel the vibration of their feelings and, for a few seconds or minutes, I have tears. I bequeath you sometimes cry for reasons you do not know.

As a child, I heard mother often use a German reason when feeling somber and I looked for tears she must have held back. "Heimweh. Heimweh." She said she was homesick. For what? She was at home. I wondered until I, too, felt mother's crying heart. Perhaps she missed her mother who died when she was one. Perhaps she missed a mother who never raised her. Perhaps she missed her father's devotion to his large family of children. Perhaps she missed a schooling she could never afford. Perhaps she missed our brother who fell. Perhaps she missed a dream that broke.

Sometimes have a longing, unfulfilled, and find the tears. A hurt can be so painful you will not cry at first. You will be brave, act as if it's not true, hold your tears, and move on. This can last for an hour, a day, or for weeks. Then you have to cry. When you cry, do not hold back. Find a room, a place, a friend, a night where you can cry. The crying will change your breathing, the way you see, your spirit, your appetite, the way you pray. After tears, I thank more, beg less, and see farther. Foliage looks greener and sky bluer; a cardinal looks brighter. I will you the gift to sometimes cry.

You have a heart for important matters. You know when something is big and counts, when something important fades, and what you will never see to the end. You know how to miss what is lost and to be overwhelmed with what cannot be changed. I bequeath you sometimes to cry. Jesus wept.

Tag

Who has not played tag? I will you the game of tag: hiding, running, touching, screaming, and laughing. I will you a game of tag: being chased, being caught, being it. I will you the joy of children being close, being far, changing spaces between each other, dodging, crawling, shouting, chasing, and running away. I will you the energy in a game of tag in full daylight.

Sometimes remember how you once played tag. I will you a game of tag at dusk, when the sun is setting, in the cool of the day, and with friends. I will you the joy of tag when the sun goes down, when darkness rises slowly, and when stars come out. I will you tag in moonlight, a time for hiding, finding another, surprising someone around a corner, being tagged. I will you joy of being seen, sought out, chased, out of breath, touched. I will you shrinking spaces, close and far, being included, being it. I know you are sometimes tagged to be it. You were touched and you are it. Sometimes you are the only one who is it. Then it will be your turn to tag another.

I will you the chance of getting your turn to run, to find another, find someone faster than you, slower, someone who wants to be it. I will you sudden times when life gets close, seems far apart, you hide, you seek, and find. There is enough to do for everyone to be it. Is it time for someone else to be it? There are times to run and not be tagged. This may not be your time to be it. Know how fast to run.

I will you tag at the end of day: one more time to touch, to phone, to laugh, one more time to be it before sleep. I will you tag after dusk, at daybreak, when you take turns being it. Touch someone in prayer, in kindness, with a cheer, with a smile. Play tag. "Seek and you will find" loved ones, saints, angels, and tomorrow.

Millie

Millie is a therapy dog. She is a handful, no more. Millie has her license and her picture on her collar, licensed to make people glad. She walks into a room as though she was raised there. She can work any hour day or night and any shift. Receptionists smile as though Millie runs the clinic. She goes in and out of hospital rooms and nursing apartments, making people well by just being a dog. Millie does what she is trained to do best, be Millie. Millie is a mentor and healer; when she enters a room, there is a glow, an aura, a fire, and a light that transfigures the place. Whose light is this?

Millie's light is the light that transfigures. There is one great light and Millie has it. Are you open to this thought? Can the light and spirit of God glow through Millie? Millie visits, listens, plays, smiles, snuggles when invited. Lisa carries her around in a cloth bag; she's hard to find unless you know she is there. She snuggles in her flannel blanket waiting for the next place to light up loneliness, darkness, and hurt. Many know her name who have forgotten their own.

I will you people who are open to the light inside beasts of creation, who enroll them in therapy school, who believe the refrain: "Millie is very good." Millie hears the whisper, "Make me well."

Do you know a Millie? She will not be painted by Michelangelo in blue, with halo, and lounging on top of a castle wall. She is not in galleries in Prague or the Metropolitan art museum. Millie is a painting in the eyes of hundreds who hear her tiny bark, "Here I am," and see her tiny feet visiting room to room. The halo is the light and the fire in faces of the people. Millie lights haloes that have eclipsed, faded, and gone out.

Sometimes Millie is a child, a caroler, a clown, a man with an accordion, and a woman with balloons. Sometimes Millie is a dog. I will you a Millie who brightens you with aura, laughter, and light.

You can hold Millie in the palm of your hands. Still, she is big enough to fill the hearts of one hundred people at once. Those who know her light see that she is very large for her size.

Hospitality

People could not tell her age or spirit. She worked hard, her hands were calloused, she often smiled, had deep-set eyes, hurried, lived on a farm, and always had an apron. I knew her spirit. She greeted every thresher by name at noontime.

She said I was a good water boy with the country threshers. I could tell it was true, for her face showed I was special, like a son. She made her kitchen a holy place and the aroma at noontime was like incense. During harvest time, being in the house of Mrs. Doetker was church. I will you her holy spirit.

I will you Mrs. Doetker's country house at noon when threshers came in to eat. She fried chicken, mashed potatoes I can still smell and taste. The gravy was like dessert. Her own pie waited for the end of the threshers' meal. I will you a good dinner with dusty farmers around a steaming table in the presence of Mrs. Doetker.

I will you more. Mrs. Doetker was a generous, helpful, kind-hearted spirit. I will you the clean white towel she gave me under the tree where I was the last to wash from a bucket on a wet bench. She willed me a clean towel. She treated me like her own. You know the feeling of belonging. That is why I bequeath you this memory of summers where you, too, were special. I will you the kindness of Mrs. Doetker, the honor, the fresh towel.

We prayed. I will you her voice when she said to the twelve men at the table, "I'm glad you came; enjoy the meal." The men believed her. I will you Mrs. Doetker who hosted thresher friends and me at her table, enjoying her hospitality in a warm summer room.

I will to you Mrs. Doetker who lived a long time ago, who greeted, graced a kitchen, gave thanks, and served the hungry. She did it all at dinner.

"For the rendering of this ministry not only supplies the needs of the saints but also overflows with many thanksgivings to God."
(2 Corinthians 9:12)

Yarmulke

Our small Christian parish was in the center of Long Island, New York. Neighbors were Jewish, synagogues plentiful, rabbis my friends. The rabbis trusted me, came to visit us, invited our family to their holy days, shared their life. I saw their yarmulke up close and wore them as I sometimes entered their places of worship. I borrowed their books, talked in their temples, joined them in brotherhood week, and witnessed their offerings for Israel. Through the years, I visited the Temple Wall, listened to their laments, and even bought a yarmulke in Jerusalem. When I wore the skullcap from time to time, I felt the warmth of God's presence on my head. I will you the yarmulke's glow of God to warm you.

I walked through the rubble of a synagogue in Berlin after the war. The guide with a red beard wore a helmet, and under it, a black yarmulke with white embroidery. From a pile of rubble, I took a tiny piece of carved stone broken by Nazi hatred and fire. Captured in this carved stone is a long and beautiful history. More than this stone, I wanted to keep the yarmulke under the hard hat. I will you a tiny piece of a people's history that may be new to you.

Then came years of workshops on worship with chaplains in the Navy. They honored me as a teacher and gifted me often. A milk pitcher from Italy, a soldier's cap, a Jewish prayer shawl, a black yarmulke. The shawl was threadbare from many years of prayer; it belonged to a rabbi's grandfather. This shawl had covered rabbis in prayer through three generations. As I held it, I joined psalmists of old and the lament of death camp alumni. More than thirty visits to Auschwitz and Buchenwald wakened the pleading of the Psalters. The yarmulke could be packed in the corner of a bag for travel, or folded into a pocket. Sometimes, I wore it where no one was present but me, and I felt the warmth of God.

The religious world is not small. God's warmth glows in many places. There are great lands we have not visited, prayer shawls we've not worn, and rituals we have still to learn. These, too, are the ways of God. I bequeath you a new piece of worship to warm you, to bless you, to make your own faith glow.

A Free Spirit

His books read like poetry, art, and paintings. As a young man, he was an artist and sculptor. In the woods, he knew leaf and sky colors and hues by heart. His walking sticks were decorated with his own designs. He was once a wood carver; now every sentence he writes has beauty. His carvings are humorous; his writing has wit. Think of someone you know whose artful spirit was never lost.

It was the year of Sputnik. Though up in years, he tried to fix his dock on Lake Zoar single-handedly. Trying to sink a very large plank just beneath the water, he sat as if riding a horse. He was not successful. All the while, he enjoyed the ride he looked into the sky singing: "I am an astronaut. I am an astronaut." I bequeath you to personally know someone gifted and witty.

His cabin ceiling had pulleys by which he could switch off lights in other rooms, from his bed. He was an inventor and could have patented his ideas. Somehow, they were tucked into the wisdom of his speaking. When early afternoon came, he napped. For seven minutes, he slept in his parked car, on the floor of a meeting room, in a hotel corridor, at a desk. He needed neither sleeping pill nor an alarm. Only seven minutes were enough wherever he was in the world at the time. I bequeath you having someone free and spontaneous at your side, able to take things as they come.

More than once I heard him lament the death of his wife. He honored her and when naming great women of history said of his own wife: "She could have done it all, herself." He often sat on the edge of his bed and wept for her. I will you someone famous who is fragile, in love, and mourns loss.

He liked apples, things simple and healthy. Before eating the apple, he studied it as though he was holding a still-life painting. While others ordered steaks and wine in hotels, he at the same table ordered one red apple. Not every hotel kitchen had a red apple, which delighted him. He was an advocate for those who are poor. He spoke out for peace. Nature was a friend. He used the same hot water to boil an egg and then shave. He picked up gloves in the street, washed them, and wore them. Most were left hand gloves; he wore them. Each leg under his dining table was taken from a discarded table. He restored what was discarded. I bequeath you the frugal nature of someone highly regarded: an author, a professor, a statesman, a saint.

When he prayed, he often looked up and winked. God was a close friend whom he trusted. He sometimes redrew his own face into woodcuts of the sixteenth century so he could live in the same time as Emperor Charles V or Martin Luther. When he needed, he phoned us in the middle of the night. I will you the friendship of a special person who trusts you and will phone you at two in the morning. Someone famous may be in need of you.

Friendship

You have a friend with whom you are completely relaxed. I do. There was a bond between Jesus and the disciple John. Did they joke, tease, test, play tricks, do a high five, show a "thumbs–up," and love comedy? Did they run races? They were friends.

I will you a friend. Tom calls me often, disguises his voice. We play like children. Sometimes he is a psychiatrist, sometimes a politician, a professor, and sometimes a stranger. The conversation resembles improvisational theater. We test each other's minds in new ways, investigating, imagining, and teasing. I will you the playfulness of a friend, regardless of age. Tom and I find this to be healing. When I have a worry, he talks me through the worry. When I laugh, he joins the laughter. We pray by phone. We have fun from a distance.

I will you a friend with whom you can be glad—a friend who keeps laughter going so you know you have laughed. You know the health in joy, laughing, the medicines released by a joyful mind. So God has made us. Consider the medicine in the Psalms and hymns of the church. The metaphors of scripture see us as grass, trees, water, storms, seed, earth, birds, and harvest. Tom has not yet called me a tree or seed or river or grass. There is humor in these biblical pictures.

You have a playful side. What I am saying is not new. Have you cherished your most playful friend? Do you nurture that relationship and feel the benefit?

The more we laugh, the more we trust. We talk about family, friend, foe. We do not hide from each other. We tell the truth about ourselves. In the middle of laughter, we reveal a worry, a hope, a dream. Suddenly I know him better; I know myself better.

I am sometimes a poet, a jester, a counselor, sometimes a bishop, or a child to him. I am playful as I was with my mother and my brother. We play heaven, angels, saints and martyrs, heroes and foes. Sometimes we are prisoners, sometimes kings. I will you the playfulness of a friend who will keep the child spirit in you alive and well.

I may have told you about a man who sometimes winks into the sky when he prays. God is his friend.

Pig

It all started with my new poem, "Love is a pig." People repeated it, wondered, looked away, laughed, and remembered it. Many learned it by heart: "Love is a pig." The poem began when I heard that if I needed a heart valve, a pig valve would be best. Therefore the poem, "Love is a pig."

My friend Malcom heard of the poem and phoned from Seattle. He told of Sven who had put off getting a plastic heart valve and was waiting to get the valve of a pig. He was sure the pig valve would be with him to his end. Malcom learned my poem by heart.

An immigrant from Latvia heard the poem. She told a long love story. She returned to her homeland and the city of Riga after fifty years. The graves of her grandparents were still well-kept.

Why? They answered, "When your parents fled Latvia fifty years ago, they gave us a pig and said, 'Keep up the graves.'" They are maintaining the graves for the sake of one pig. She now knows the pig poem in Latvian. I will you a pig poem that is true, which people understand, and memorize. Someone learned it in Poland.

Hospital chaplains had a retreat. "Love is a pig" was their theme. They know that pig metabolism is similar to the human. They know about the pig heart valve. Each told a pig story, each learned the poem, "Love is a pig." The story is about a life laid down for another.

Sacrificial life has long been honored by people of God. Jesus knew poems like "Love is an ox." "Love is a turtle dove." "Love is a lamb." What is it I will you? Honor all that is a sacrifice for you. Honor people and beasts and martyrs who lay down life for us.

I am sure you are respectful of sacrifice. You have seen lives given and spent for you. You have read of lives laid down for yourself. The poem I love most is, "Love is a lamb." I think of the paschal lambs, and the Lamb John pointed to saying, "Behold the Lamb of God." Love that is unconditional is sacrificial. Love can be felt toward a sheep, a guinea pig, a pig, a martyr. I will you a love song for some creature of God that gives you life. I will you the poem: "Love is a Pig." Love is a Friend. Love is sacrificial.

Valentine

I will you a secret poem; a valentine never sent; a few lines hid in the earth, under grass, five feet west of the evergreen.

I will you a secret message in the West Wall of Jerusalem, one word behind a medieval altar in Magdeburg, Germany. Write a song and plant it with the next rosebush. "Roses bloom red, yellow, or white; my heart starts blooming when you are in sight." Write a loving secret, plant it in the earth, know it is there. Let roots consume the poem, smell the love in the leaves, feel the touch in the bloom. You know romance; you know the power of love. I will you a kind word, hid somewhere forever, like a treasure chest in the deep sea.

Find a tiny phrase you like. Believe it, feel it, and say it when someone you love is near. Hide a loving poem inside yourself. Say it to yourself, feel how it feels when you believe it, and when you do not say it aloud. What are the ways to grow your love?

Find one word to whisper into the night sky, one song to sing alone, together. Imagine painting a valentine in the dark, by heart, when no one is near. I will you a poem you like, that you wish you had written. Put it in a special place. Remember where you put it; read it when you need to. Keep alive a good word by hiding it so it will always be there.

My friend Karl had wine in his basement that his wife made. Nine years ago, she died. Karl goes there to drink a toast. He did not share the drink with me. He savors it. I will you a private place when you, too, are fragile, to go to visit. Make it your sanctuary. Go there to be special.

I am finding love notes Lois and I wrote each other in the past fifty-eight years. I believe she saved and hid some to be found. She has died; I am finding them. Make a valentine for someone to find someday. You know how it feels to find an old valentine. In the center of all Scripture, you will find a steadfast valentine waiting to be found.

Prayer

Pray. Listen around, and hear how others pray. I will you the power of praying. Yesterday in the airport, I was riding the cart because I could not walk to the gate. I lamented. The driver from Nigeria listened and said his first words to me: "Just pray." I felt better the rest of the trip. I still feel the power of his praying words. He admonished me like Paul in letters to his churches.

I bequeath you, sometimes, just pray. Francis would not let anyone take a bite or pass the food. Age five he sat in control, though he had tasted a piece of cheese, and asked his father to sit down. I will always hear his sentence: "First, we have to pray."

Zoe, age four, came to the table with a new prayer printed on a card. We all read the words. She knew them by heart. She led the praying: "Thank you, Jesus, for this food. Amen." It was Thanksgiving. With the same new prayer, she led other dinners that day. That sentence was enough Thanksgiving for all, for me, and for many to come. Her prayer has stayed in me. Sometimes, keep the prayer of a child in you and repeat it. One sentence is long enough.

When very young, I memorized two lengthy prayers in German. Since then, hardly a night has passed when I did not sing and pray one or both. The pictures of safety, protection, and peace I received seventy-five years ago are a devotion I still feel. The child in me still finds peace in prayer. I bequeath you the miraculous pictures of a childhood prayer. You know the prayers you once said by heart. Refresh them and trust their continued strength.

I have written several thousand prayers through the years. Many have been hymns, and greetings in letters. A single sentence prayer at the end of a visit, story, argument, day, tragedy, or surprise may be your best ending. Sometimes find one sentence that says it all. One word can be a mantra. A lengthy creed, Lord's Prayer, or the Doxology said every day at a certain time can be calming. Sometimes a prayer sounds better when it has weathered. Emma often said "Amen" in the midst of everything else, when there was a pause. Some say "Amen" aloud in worship. Some feel it while watching children at play or the ten o'clock news. In my lifetime while listening to world news, I have often whispered "Hear us and help us, O Lord."

How often I saw tears in Lois's eyes when the news reported children being harmed. I knew they would be prayed for before she went to sleep. I bequeath you to pray continually. Make all things known unto God—all things.

"The prayer of the righteous is powerful and effective."
(James 5:16)

Dove

Pastor David liked extraordinary worship, kept simple. The real world was the language of God, even a homing pigeon.

For communion, he liked bread with aroma. In baptism, you could hear water splash. During Lent, there was a rock or waterfall or lamb in the chancel. On this night of Lent, five hundred met again for their journey to Easter. David brought a white dove into the sanctuary, which was no surprise to us. He gave me the homing dove plus five minutes to prepare its journey into the night.

You know people who do something unusual once and it becomes a legend. David is a legend whom I have been glad to assist in these unique moments of worship. Being with a homing dove is awesome in a Lenten night. We sang, prayed, talked of spirit and beloved. We considered the dove. I do not remember all that was said. I remember the walk up the church aisle, into a crowded parking lot, the clouded sky in a stormy night, and the wind. All kept their eyes on the dove. David held fast to the dove now named Spirit. On the count of three, David let go and Spirit hurried home into the storm.

I bequeath you letting a homing dove fly for its home. I will you a dove that will soon fly a journey it is called to go. Feel the longing inside, the Geiger-counter, and the dove's heart race. Oh, the cold wind; Spirit hunted a path inside the wind, scribbled a way into the night air, and scaled the clouds. There was no direction for the path of Spirit.

I will you hunting the path for your own spirit journey and believing you will find the way. The path was in the wind; the path was in the dove. The white dove memorized the stormy wind and sky and then found a power of what seemed to be a jet stream. Spirit was looking for a way in the sky. Twenty miles northeast was home. Spirit found a way home inside the tumbling currents of wind. Spirit used the strength of a storm, wind under wings to journey back home. A windy breath was the power of the flight. I will you the strength of wind inside a storm to find the path to home.

I will you Spirit, a dove in the wind. There was a dove over the Jordan; come down as Spirit to show Jesus a ministry path. Jesus understood the sign of a dove.

"O that I had wings like a dove! I would fly away and be at rest."
(Psalm 55:6)

Unfinished Business

"Then the righteous will answer him, 'Lord, when was it that we saw you hungry and gave you food, or thirsty and gave you something to drink? And when was it that we saw you a stranger and welcomed you, or naked and gave you clothing? And when was it that we saw you sick or in prison and visited you?' And the king will answer them, 'Truly I tell you, just as you did it to one the least of these who are members of my family, you did it to me.'" (Matthew 25:37-40)

"Little children, I am with you only a little longer. You will look for me; and as I said to the Jews so now I say to you, 'Where I am going, you cannot come.' I give you a new commandment, that you love one another. Just as I have loved you, you also should love one another. By this everyone will know you are my disciples, if you have love for one another." (John 13:33-35)

O the thirst inside the rivers,
Fountains looking for the deep;
Hear the children in the deserts:
Thirsty, thirsty while they weep.
Hear them, hear them; it is Jesus.
Jesus knows the silent song.
Jesus knows the helpless sorrow
When the water is all gone.

Palaces and all with riches
Have their thirst and need a cup.
Movie stars and baseball heroes
Need, O Lord, be lifted up.
Presidents, all queens, and soldiers,
All who stand beside a brink,
Hold a cup and need a blessing,
Have a thirst and need your drink.
Hymn: I Thirst

Christmas Tree

Our Christmas tree has sometimes stayed standing on the patio until April. In January, it became an Epiphany tree with stars, in February, a Valentine tree with hearts, then a Lenten tree with crosses. It is April: the tree still stands on the patio, wanting to bear gifts. I will you a Christmas tree that does not quit; which stays, goes on bringing joy, and connects the birth in Bethlehem with all holy feasts. I will you to know what may stay.

This is not a gift to bequeath to all. I bequeath it to you. I play Christmas music all year. It is hard for me to quit a season, toss a tree, discard a pair of old shoes, or close a book.

How is it with you? You know best how long you can keep a tree standing. Now the tree is a feeding place, and shelters birds in cold winter. Birds are decorating the very dry tree with their presence. Cardinals are flying into the tree with string and sticks and dried grasses. The nest will be perfect. They work, they sing. They have found the favorite tree for a cardinal nest, a spruce. I will you befriending a cardinal in an old Christmas tree. The branches are dry, the stems stiff. It is a tree of dry, sharp needles in which birds have found a home. All neighbors' Christmas trees are long in some city dump. Ours is nesting cardinals.

Sometimes, let something stay a while and become a new thing. Sometimes save something you intend to throw away. See what happens. I will you a Christmas tree in April, still standing on a patio, dry needles, brown, trimmed once more by two birds, nesting.

Nothing is finished when the Christmas season is over. Advent begins the church year. All the seasons come to play tag. Sometimes see that Christmas is never over, nor is Easter.

"Be prepared in season and out of season." (2 Timothy 4:2 NIV)

Peace Work

Sixty years ago, I drove through the rubble of cities and country-sides delivering lard, flour, clothing, and sugar to refugees after World War II. I can still see the laughter and tears in faces of women, children, and men around my Jeep. To them, I was like a celebrity. Bouquets of flowers crowded my car for the ride home. Waving hands filled the sky. That year taught me a lesson about peace. Making peace has to do with sharing and touching and food and drink and clothing. I will you the making of peace.

There was more to do. Students came from five nations to repair a burned cathedral. On Palm Sunday, firebombs brought down the great bells of St. Mary's, where Buxtehude and Bach had often played together. We read, studied, shoveled, dug, and lifted until at the end of each day we were tired and glad. I will you the gladness of being tired making peace.

Five years later, I joined thirty young people to shovel rubble from a great city, to separate toys from broken bricks, and to build a road from the rubble. More important were the songs we shared, our stories, our feelings. We met friends of Dietrich Bonhoeffer, learned about grace and hope and forgiveness, sang spirituals and old canons. We prayed, sweated, listened, danced—and built a road together. The rubble road is in us. I will you the joy of building roads of peace with enemies and warlords and victims.

You are among those who believe in the industry of peace; you will make peace with energy. Your heart is open to a legacy of toiling over peace. Remember the peace work you have done. See the faces and places you have made peaceful. You know that *shalom* is active, dusty, hungry, sweaty, energizing, musical, inquisitive work.

I will you the heart and sweat of peace work.

> *"Blessed are the peacemakers, for they will be called*
> *children of God." (Matthew 5:9)*

Crushed Pencil

"O look, another broken pencil." For years, I bent to pick up broken, crushed pencils, mostly in parking lots, where cars had broken their wood and lead. The pencil could still write a song, a poem, a letter, a litany. I have given many crushed pencils with a new song to people in the world. Children are amazed and glad that a broken pencil still has a song to write. I will you a crushed pencil. You know the broken feeling, and there is still a song to write.

People who feel deeply wounded understand the writings of the crushed pencil. Prisoners don't need an explanation. Jesus taught in ways that persons felt the message. When is anything done, over, finished? You think about that. A fallen limb is not done. Our hillside woods are filled with fallen wood. The branches can be a bonfire, mulch, and a ground cover in heavy rains. Broken things still have a song inside. A maple grown from seed was six feet high. Quickly we transplanted it; too quickly. It died. The root is now the crook of a walking stick. With care, it will be here in fifty years. You know how a sudden death can crush a whole person and family. For a while, the broken pieces lie as in a heap, and we stare at life as though even the lead is gone. Slowly, alone, one by one, together we stoop to pick up the broken pencil and we find a song we did not write before. We do the same with a person.

Winter is only a season. Perennials and annuals are not stopped by a sudden freeze. I will you the words of a crushed song you had no time to write, a tune no one has heard. I will you the cherishing of a dream born out of pain. I will you spring after winter.

I have felt the crush of a pencil lost in a dusty parking lot. You know the feeling of wounds that would break you to disuse. It can happen with illness, age, lost love, death. In that broken hour, I have written cantatas, sent a kind note, said a prayer, and made reconciliation. In such a time, bake a good cake, wrap a special gift, find a bouquet, make a cup of tea, and walk across a room to say a right word.

Trees That Made It

Don just wrapped my maple tree for the winter. Deer tore the bark from hunger last year. The tree wept and lives. The deer will not harm it this winter. A pine tree planted for a wedding has grown bent. It is staked and will be straight. Three spruce have struggled through a dry summer. Friends have helped keep the roots watered. The tops are dry and will be pruned. Two will make it, perhaps all three. The ash seed grew on its own. We did not plant it among the oaks. Its long thin trunk has pierced the open sky and the top is bright green. It made it.

The boy in Beijing could not walk. A therapist showed his parents and nurses how to teach him. The therapist returned after three years and I was there. The boy walked into the room on his own. She had promised he would. Doctors said Doris would not live long; the surgery was radical. Thirty years later, she was still at her desk in the church, making phone calls. You know how it is to hope, pray, encourage, and to see something broken mend.

A child had polio; it was the time of the iron lung. He would always stay connected to the iron box, the doctor said. His mother said he would walk. He did, with crutches. He learned to use his hands. His feet learned to do what they had not done before. He opened his own carpenter's shop. He made it.

The young man was an addict, then a thief, a robber. He was in prison. Now he is a father, a dear husband, he sings hymns, does good. He made it. Now he helps his son who is in prison. The father says the son will make it.

I will you trees that will make it. I will you what is broken or bent or withered or dying. You are the kind of person who can tie it straight, wrap it safe, hold it in your arms, sing it a song, see it get well.

Bells

I will you the bell that calls children in from play, to home. A bell the child knows by heart; like the voice of a mom or dad calling. A bell that says: time to eat, time to go to bed, time to read a book, time for chores. Lois and I loved ringing a bell in the valley when our family was young. It was evening; they came running for dinner, warmth, and story telling. Our bell had its own tone.

How do you remember your childhood bell? Do you remember a bell that called you in from recess? Can you smell the room as children gather after running and playing hard in a warm school day, the bell still ringing? Bells have a sound and an aroma. I bequeath you the sound of a bell saying come in, come home, time for dinner.

For a while, our cat wore a bell. The birds heard and flew away just in time. The cat did not seem to know the bell was preventing the catch. It stayed in the hunt day after day never catching a bird. Catching a bird stayed a dream. The bird was saved by the bell.

A radio program began with the ringing of a bell. I loved the sound. The ringing was what I needed to get near the radio. In later years, I traveled to another land with sponsors of the radio program. We each took a bell and at historic sites rang our bells as a choir and did something memorable. The bells called us to a holy act. I will you a bell sound that feels special and sacred.

When I hear the bells of a fire engine going by, I am transported to church. I pray thoughts of intercession, protection, and guidance. The fire engine calls me to prayer. You know the same feeling. I bequeath you to keep that sense alive.

My first visit to the Alps had bells in it, cows somewhere on a hillside munching, looking for greener grass, heading home. Alfred Hecker in Nebraska had a bell on his lead cow. Alfred shouted "Com' Boss," and Bessie led all her cows home. We could hear the bell with every step; the herd followed. A shepherd had a bell. The bell rang and sheep came running.

You know the sound of bells. You know your own bells by heart. Perhaps you know a sleigh with bells, or bells on a holiday door, or a crib toy, or a fire engine. I bequeath you the voice of a bell that for a while calls you into a good world, or all the way home. There is something about a bell.

Hymn: "Jesus Is Calling" (first verse)
Softly and tenderly, Jesus is calling,
Calling for you and for me;
See, on the portals he's waiting and watching,
Watching for you and for me.

Refrain
Come home, come home,
You who are weary, come home;
Earnestly, tenderly, Jesus is calling,
Calling, O sinner, come home!
(Will L. Thompson)

Log

A log fell over a creek. We had a bridge to walk over—a strong bridge without a rail. We walked the bridge with care. It was a challenge in rain, but it was the only way to cross the creek. I will you an ordinary log that is sometimes slippery, but is your way to the other side.

A professor was known for making students thoughtful. In class, he engaged a student so that the student felt they were side by side at two ends of a single log. He became known as the professor who taught on a log. With him, learning was head to head, heart to heart, toe to toe, face to face. He was often a tutor, a friend on a log.

You have learned with such a person. You sat side by side on a single log, on a bench, on a church pew, or across from each other in a café. You have been on the same log or in the same place with mentors who taught you heart to heart. I bequeath you a log for learning. Meet a friend in a humble place and learn.

A log leans against a great oak in our woods. For sixty years, it was the arm of a great oak. Now, examining the log up close, I see nests bored deep in the wood that housed birds of all kinds. There beneath the sky, woodpeckers found their food. The log showed the strength of their beaks. Now I see what I heard in their pecking through the years. The log stores years of stories. Look carefully at some fallen log. See what only birds nesting and resting knew. Watch a log in winter, when in blowing snow it shelters a cottontail or a warming pheasant. I will you a common log to see and photograph and stir warm feelings in a cold winter storm. It is good to have pity from a warm room for a bird hunting shelter in a winter wind, or nesting in April. It is good to see beauty, close up, and feel pity.

My friend took a log and made breadboards. His name is on thousands of them. They are in kitchens around the world.

You know logs that fed a campfire. You know logs that made a raft, sailed a swamp, and fed a fireplace. Our favorite birch tree died. How precious the wood, dressed in Minnesota white. We savored the logs for holidays in our Franklin stove. We savored wood we moved through three states, which now holds earth and perennials on a hillside. The log and the plants are friends. They are like the professor who taught students on a log. A simple log can bridge two worlds, two minds, two sides of a creek, or shelter a bird in a storm. I will you a log.

A Thought

Ten years ago, I had this thought that has not left me. It is now a dream and I will not finish it. I am sure you have unfinished thoughts that were profound to you and you want someone to know the dream.

My thought caught hold of me while walking through a hospital complex in India. Some day singers, a choir, must walk slowly through a hospital complex, not only in India, but everywhere in the third world, or at home where you live, singing, healing, comforting. Most choirs keep their eyes on the conductor. This choir will sing with eyes on the people; seeing their eyes while they sing. The complex we walked through had many beds out in the open. Patients and families looked at us, into our faces, our eyes. You know the feeling of an audience, looking at you, hopefully, expectantly. If you ever sang in a choir you know how persons felt your voices and the harmony, saw your feelings, took your spirit into their eyes. Could your choir walk through a hospital? I will you a healing choir singing your best, eyes on the people, making every patient feel like being in the first row.

I was so fixed on faces I almost stumbled over beds. One woman caught my eyes in the hospital complex. She might have been forty, or eighty. Her concern for her child drew me to her side. I felt I heard her whisper: "Make my little one well. Be her medicine in music." I will you this healing dream born one hot summer in a large compassionate south India hospital. You know the wish: "Make me well." I bequeath some woman and child waiting for you to sing to them.

Wherever we went, the people knew we were there. We stepped out of the bus and there was an audience. Had we sung, these poor people would have listened. I bequeath you to make singing a medicine for hundreds who cannot pay. Join those who believe in the miracle of music. Sing without a stage. Sing unannounced, without posters and advertising. Sing to heal others, sing to make yourself well; let their faces and amazement heal you. Surprise them softly. I will you this thought of mine: a musical healing journey. The dream is not dead. It is not too late for you find some way to do this thought of mine.

I will you a thought I began and cannot finish. You know the game of tag. Now you are it. Now the dream is yours. Perhaps you can finish the thought. If not, give it to another; someday it will happen.

Jesus said: "What do you want me to do for you?" The blind beggar said he wanted to see again. Jesus healed him, "and all the people, when they saw it, praised God" (Luke 18:41-43). Find someone who needs healing and hope; someone for you to sing to.

Dance

I will you a dance. I will you being with someone you love, dancing to music you like, a time you will remember. Country folks I knew said Ida danced at weddings. I wanted to stay to see a dance, to see her dance. Her right leg was short from polio. People said Ida danced well. I will you to see Ida dance.

Our family did not dance. Ministers' families were not supposed to dance. Mother knew when the dancing would begin; she gave father a sign, and we were on our way to the car. All the way home, I imagined dancing in a dance I never saw.

Ida sang alto in our little choir. When Ida walked down the aisle she did not limp; she danced. To me, her walk was a dance. I saw dancing when the people who danced on Saturdays walked down the aisle to their seat on Sunday. I saw them dancing the prelude played by Lydia, dancing with open hymnals, dancing the Gloria. The meter and rhythm of the hymns were like the dance I did not hear Saturday night. I looked at Ida singing alto as she harmonized with soprano voices. It was a dance, two voices different, dancing a song together.

I will you seeing a dance in holy places, and feeling holiness in dancing. When the choir stood to sing, I imagined Lydia the organist, now sixteen, also dancing. She too had polio. At the organ, I could not see her feet dancing. I do not know how she danced at weddings. During "Holy, Holy, Holy" and "Abide with me," Lydia danced every line. So did Ida and the soprano section and my father and all the people. We danced the way David the singer "danced before the LORD with all of his might" (2 Samuel 6:14). I will you the fun of dance. A dance moves inside us; it is the spirit of God in us.

Potato

We learned about trust in our garden. I really believed when Lois planted any flower. When little faith grew when I planted potatoes. I trusted; they grew. In the garden, we practiced believing. I put a tomato seed into a half shell, then water, then offered it light through a window. I believed it would grow. I will you simple trust. Dig it up to look; it will quit growing. I did. I was seven. Trust that seed will grow with earth, light, and water. Sow and wait.

My bantam hen clucked and sat on her tiny speckled eggs for exact days she knew by heart. She knew just when to roll them, when to peck them open for the chicks to escape. I broke one open to look, to be sure it was alive. It was too soon. It did not live. I will you the patience of a hen that will wait and wait and trust. When eggs do not hatch, the hen will start over. She keeps on believing.

I built trust as a boy playing in the pasture: it was the wind and the kite. I knew wind would carry my kite high above the field if I ran into the wind. Run into the wind and watch the kite rise, twist, turn, climb, and climb. Believe the wind will do it. Trust a kite will fly if you know how to use the wind. Once a kite was too heavy and a friend cut it in half. It flew. If making something smaller works, make it little. Trust a kite can fly if you cut it in half.

You know ways to build trust. Look around in the garden, fly kites, watch potatoes, see friends believing. Trust is inscribed in us. I bequeath you the wisdom to learn trust, to pray for patience to see seeds break through, to trust pain to heal, to trust faith to grow. Trust the wind to do it. Trust.

Once we planted potatoes in a large garden. A candle in the center made it an altar. We waited. The altar flowers bloomed: white and yellow, the way potatoes bloom.

Trust is a gift from God. The sun will set. Dusk will come, then dark, then dawn. The earth and potato, the kite and wind, a friend with me all help in my trusting God. We do not trust alone. God is about building trust. That is what Jesus does for me: holds everything together so I trust.

"Holding fast to the head . . . the whole body, nourished and held together by its ligaments and sinews, grows with a growth that is from God." (Colossians 2:19)

Those Who Are Poor

If only I had spent a few minutes with Mother Teresa. She would have taken me to those who are very poor, and to God. I will you time with the poorest of the poor. I will you to know one mother in a hospital complex, seated on the ground beside a child's bed. I saw her from a distance; she saw me up close. Find that mother. Sing her child one song to be well. Let her see you seeing her, knowing her child is there.

I will you to eat with those who are homeless. I watched them sleeping in cardboard boxes in winter. There were five boxes before a cathedral door. Perhaps you have seen them.

I will you mothers who stand beside touring buses and press hungry babies against windows for you to see. I will you to get off a bus in Calcutta, meet a mother, hold her child. I will you boys who walk on all fours like spiders, begging, hands outstretched for help, pleading in a language we do not comprehend. I will you the poorest of poor in Bulgaria; the woman who stared for ten minutes at one man eating ice cream. He finally gave her a half eaten cone, bowed, and left. I will you this woman, poor and persistent.

Have you visited those who are very poor? Do you know their stories, their jokes, for what they thank, what they want most? I bequeath you those who are very poor near you. Walk a street where you do not live. See young who feel poor, act poor, are poor. I will you these who wait for one kind word from you.

I will you those who would touch the hem of your dress, your sleeve, your slacks if they could. They believe you will make them better, make them well. Go near them slowly so they may see you, touch you. Find ways to touch, hear. I will you with your own eyes to see young with swollen bellies, flies sucking water at their eyes, a smile for a single bag of wheat flour. I will you to hear their gratitude for one slice of bread, one cup of powdered milk, one bowl of soup. I will you to bless the poorest of poor. You will find God there.

> *"Has not God chosen the poor in the world to be rich in faith and to be heirs of the kingdom that he has promised to those who love him?" (James 2:5)*

Cleaning Lady

I will you the lady at a bus stop in South Chicago. It could be a stop in Cleveland, Raleigh, Omaha, Denver. This stop is in Chicago, Illinois. I will you the woman waiting for the next bus, on her way to where a credit card cannot take you. She will go through a high door, down the corridor, to many corners in toilets and kitchens and basements and bus depots to clean. She is a cleaning lady with a silver bucket and a blue rag from her old dress, certified to work. She has no plastic card with an expiration date. She has enough work for today. The blue rag is frayed, her hands more worn than last year, she is still humming, and her feet are tired.

I will you the woman with the silver bucket whose name I do not know; famous for cleaning corridors and closets and wiping furniture. For now, she lives in Chicago. I will you a cleaning woman who is famous in any city where corners need to be clean and kindergarten rest rooms must meet state standards.

There is no CEO looking for her work and she will not lose her job even if they lower her pay. She is not on a ladder moving upward. In thirty minutes, she will be on her knees with soap and a wet blue cloth cleaning every corner before the people come. I will you the early bird who catches a worm at minimum pay, who thanks God while on her knees scrubbing, who sings a song by heart that her mother taught her.

I will you to watch a lady waiting for the bus to take her to a high office or a hotel suite or bus depot toilet to do what few are qualified to do. She is president of her company, sometimes the only one in her corporation, and reports directly to God. I will you the woman with the blue rag and the silver bucket, waiting for the bus before sunrise and back on the same bus after sunset to make dinner.

You know this woman, who is sometimes a man. That is why I bequeath you this person who does not require a credit card to live. She has a bucket and a blue rag and a song. There is wealth only those who are poor possess. I pray that you find those who are poor, and that they find you.

Renaissance Persons

Renaissance people make old things new. They break open hope, value, and worth. They waken the spirit of God in people. I will you John and Bobbie. He paints. She weaves. They create patterns, seek beauty, feed cardinals, wave to sunsets, and plant seed. I will you people who see twice. One sees a landscape and sketches large murals. One sees a child and weaves a poncho. I will you the art of looking at one thing, reflecting, creating another, and more. Why? Because you are a renaissance person and may not know it.

They bought ninety acres, stood on a hill, looked at the land, had a dream, and began the dream. Together, looking at the expanse of plowed field they saw a forest. I will you a forest on an open plowed field. They looked at their own past years. The woods had disappeared. They saw the empty field, and looked ahead. They closed their eyes and dreamed new woods of trees. They agreed to turn the open field into a forest of ninety acres. I will you to make a place more beautiful, more fruitful.

They walked fields and front yards and parks to find acorns, walnuts, apple seed, ash, maple. Friends heard of the forest and helped find seed. Bobbie and John would plant a forest they may never see. I will you to plant a forest you will not see. Seed came from a hundred places. Children's children will inherit woods of white oak, red oak, larch, walnut, burr, elm, basswood, and apple. September came, they scattered baskets of seed in the great plowed field, all the while dreaming, seeing saplings, seedlings, giant trees, a forest. They see the years ahead: families at play, children finding walnuts, a bonfire of broken limbs, birds in nests, raccoons in the night, owls, deer, autumn colors. They blessed the seed.

I will you sowing a legacy. I will you trees you plant, seed you scatter, land you decorate, earth you love. Generations will bless you. I will you anonymity, doing good for goodness sake, loving for love sake, painting and weaving for beauty sake, one tree, one weaving, one rug, silent gifts. I will you planting a tree you will not see, sowing what you will not harvest, and making bread you will not eat.

If you do not plant a tree, plant a thought, a way of life, a home, a sign of faith, an act of love. I will you Bobbie and John and a forest they have begun. Martin Luther was asked what he would do if he knew the world would end. His answer: "I would plant a tree." A tree planted is a sign of hope.

Dried Daisies

I was to be speaker at a men's banquet. Of course, I wanted the men to remember the night and to think about what I said, what I did, and what they thought. It was winter. I went outside and cut three dried daisies and put them into the pocket near my lapel. I will you a boutonniere of dried daisies. Lois was not surprised and would be eager to hear what the men said when I came home.

Lest I crush them, I did not cover them with an overcoat. As I stopped at red lights, people looked at me wondering about the dried boutonniere in my coat. I acted as though I didn't notice. Upon arriving, I found the banquet room filled with men snacking on cheese, crackers, and wine. I entered with my dried daisies and greeted them—some friends, most of them strangers. They were kind and carried on conversation as usual. No one mentioned the daisies. I bequeath you the art of surprising without offending.

We had dinner and the program ran as usual. My daisies were very prominent and covered my entire lapel. It was not that the men did not see the boutonniere. They just didn't know what to say.

I do not remember my theme but it must have had something to do with life. Toward the end of my talk I said: "Perhaps you noticed my boutonniere." A man I did not know hollered: "It's dead!" He shouted; though his voice was full of astonishment and curiosity. Why would the speaker be wearing something dead? I asked what he had said, and again he shouted: "It's dead!"

I did not answer; paused a moment, took the seed into my hands and crushed them. Then I walked past the men, one by one, and gave them some seed, saying, "Take, and sow. Take, and sow." That was the end of my talk. I concluded with a postscript, "When you think it's dead, it ain't." I will you the surprise hidden in a seed.

"Very truly, I say to you, unless a grain of wheat falls into the earth and dies, it remains just a single grain; but if it dies, it bears much fruit." (John 12:24)

Decorating Seasons

I will you a creative spirit, a poetic heart; I will you feeling long ago and today at once, far away and here and now. I will you decorating old seasons of faith with places and people and trees and hillsides and accidents and wars you know. I bequeath you the wonderful feeling of truth that wakes deep in the imagination of the heart with startling contrasts and comparisons. These often begin with the help of, "Once upon a time." I am writing in the Christmas season, but any season has its now moments.

Once upon a time, a church of very good people wanted to learn a new way to make Christmas Eve interesting. The church had used many plays and often sung carols.

Some felt Christmas Eve was losing its meaning. The council voted to project television news on a giant screen while singing carols and reading the gospel.

During the singing of "Joy to the World," they heard people in a great city crying in the midst of a great storm, and it was Christmas Eve. In a southern state, a frost came far too early for oranges and blossoms, people were making fires in orchards, and it was Christmas Eve. In a little northern town, sun had melted a sculpted ice show, and it was Christmas Eve. On a steep hillside where children had gathered to slide, rain poured hard and houses washed into thick mud, and it was Christmas Eve. On the way to church, a family died in an accident, and it was Christmas Eve.

In Ohio, a woman died of cancer; and it was Christmas Eve. While a town was decorating their trees, a tornado tore through their rooms, scattered their gifts in the air, and it was Christmas Eve. While singing "Silent Night," it was reported in the world that some were caught caroling in a storm, some were kneeling in mud, babies were crying for milk, bombs were bursting in a war, a mother lost her child, and it was still Christmas Eve.

The church learned that it may not be necessary to buy Christmas programs. Christmas comes with a program. Christmas comes in storm, in cold, in heat, in quake, in death, in poverty, in birth. God makes Christmas come wherever. The kingdom of heaven is of God.

A World to Come

"Nothing accursed will be found there any more. But the throne of God and of the Lamb will be in it, and his servants will worship him; they will see his face and his name will be on their foreheads. And there will be no more night; they need no light of lamp or sun, for the Lord God will be their light, and they will reign for ever and ever" (Revelation 22:3-5).

Thine the glory in the night, no more dying, only light.
Thine the river, thine the tree, then the Lamb eternally.
Then the holy, holy, holy celebration jubilee,
Thine the splendor, thine the brightness, only thee, only thee.
Hymn: Thine the Amen, Thine the Praise

Talk with us, till we behold
A joyful life you will unfold:
Heal our eyes to see the prize:
Jesus take us to the light.
Hymn: Stay with Us

Death Camp

In Buchenwald, I experienced hope.

In the past thirty years, I have visited Buchenwald and Auschwitz death camps more than thirty times. I have seen piles of shoes, leg and body braces, tons of hair, suitcases with names and numbers painted in large letters, and children's clothing. I have read posters of racism, persecution, holocaust, and death. We have cried, viewing paintings by prison children; the paintings and poems once buried in mother earth now hang in galleries in Prague. The lamenting of the innocent still cries. Prayers of all faiths cling in display to old barracks. We have sat in the grasses of Birkenau beside a single blossom and heard their hope. I will you hope found in the presence of a single blossom gracing a silent saddened meadow.

We watched a butterfly flutter past old beds once stacked with sleeping, frightened, starving, dying. We read imprecatory and hopeful psalms. The butterfly woke our spirits. Once, prisoners were empowered by the sight of a single bird, a butterfly, a shadow of cloud, and a wisp of wind. With choirs, we stood in death camps and sang anthems without voicing a sound. The music was still as death, each word and tune unspoken. The song was consumed in silence. We listened to what was unsung, dedicating a silent hymn to unsung songs. We felt wind and spirit fill the air. We and saints were together in the wind of God, and there was no power that would destroy us. Resurrection and life filled the hillside of Buchenwald. Everything was one. I will you the spirit of God blowing over dry bones and cemeteries and promising resurrection.

You know the places where hope is born, where death is wakened, where seed blooms, and dry bones wake. I bequeath you life in places of death.

Often, we consecrated bread and wine, drank and ate some. We poured the rest in the grass of the camp, remembering the hungry and thirsty. In Ravensbruck, we dug holes, planted our dinners in memory of mothers and children who died of hunger, and then planted trees. Pray, sing, visit, stay in hard places until you remember you have been there. Be with those who are hungry, sick, poor, imprisoned. Jesus made compassion a law. I will you the rule of love, the law of compassion, and the wind of hope. I bequeath you silent places of great hope.

"Suffering produces endurance, and endurance produces character, and character produces hope." (Romans 5:3-4)

Aftermath

For months, I witnessed old women in a war-torn nation cleaning rubble, piling stones on stones of once famous boulevards and buildings. This was the beginning after a terrible ending. You know the aftermath of wars, of death, of tornadoes, of floods. That is why I bequeath you new beginnings after endings of hurt.

There have been many aftermaths since World War II. You know them. One is this: the earth is planted with millions of land mines. I will you the careful feet of those treading like fog through land mines, searching, saving legs and arms of children at play. I will you the aftermath of cities angry, nations ruined, feelings torn, families divided, and spirits tormented. You know of aftermath, the months and years and decades that follow catastrophes.

I will you planting gardens where there were high walls, rows of trees where there were mines, making a path lined with violets where tanks did tread the earth, and setting a table where there was a bomb shelter. I will you visiting men and women wounded who will not sing, will not hope, and will not to live. Many will hope if you sing, you love, and you hope with them. I will you the aftermath of treaties where dignitaries shake hands, agree, sign promises, and need all the people to do the peace that passes understanding.

I will you the aftermath of death where grief cries out, injustice seeks revenge, and the only way ahead is reconciliation. I will you the miracle of peace and forgiveness and justice and beauty and breaking bread and creating a family to embrace the enemy. I will you the aftermath of what is evil and will only heal with your own good will.

I bequeath you a world where we no longer sort rubble, clean bricks, and begin over and over. And if there is rubble or a flood, go help clean the bricks, plant a garden, shovel trash, hold hands, practice hope, sing a good song.

"For I am about to create new heavens and a new earth; the former things shall not be remembered." (Isaiah 65:17)

A Trunk

I will you a beautiful trunk, strapped in copper, old, and locked. I will you a locked trunk with no key. Thirty youth and I went to the Savage, Minnesota city dump to claim throw-aways. The retreat was for practicing compassion. Two boys found a trunk on which they practiced pity. I will you a friend who finds a locked trunk with you, helps carry it all day wherever you go, and talks with you about a treasure inside.

Why do we love intrigue? What is there about mystery? I will you a treasure locked inside an old trunk with no key. For eight hours, I saw two keep close watch, guarding the mystery of a locked trunk with their lives. Mystery is at the heart of prayer. Mystery is at the heart of holy days. I will you the mystery of what is precious because you know mystery: the mystery of birth, of music, of miracles, of forgiveness, of a friend.

The two were speechless with excitement most of the day. The priceless locked trunk had been rescued from a dump. I will you something thrown away, discarded, left behind, hiding a mystery. The day was finished, students pondered compassion, the sun was setting, the trunk stayed locked. Thirty gathered on the hill, quiet as in prayer, expecting, and facing the locked trunk. The trunk was now their altar. I will you gathering around a mystery with friends, hoping, quietly, for a sacred moment. The lock was rusted; a prize inside would be old. I will you old prizes locked for decades, for thousands of years, diamonds in sunken ships, and scrolls in clay pots.

On a silent count of three, the lid was pried, broken open, lifted. There was the prize. Empty. Empty. Some regretted. The two finder's faces burst into laughter, pure delight, and joy. They had found the prize of the locked trunk. They had the treasure: the waiting, the expectation. The compassion led to waiting, and to wakening of hope. Finding nothing, they had found everything. For eight hours, they had renewed hope. As they stayed with the rusted, locked trunk, their hope grew. I will you the gift of expectation, waiting, hoping. I will you an empty trunk, left behind, locked, with no key.

Love what you have found. I will you friends to be with you when you have found something discarded, precious, locked. Once builders tossed away a stone that became a cornerstone. His name is Jesus.

"Have you never read in the scriptures: The stone that the builders rejected has become the cornerstone?" (Matthew 21:42)

Hourglass

When Beth was born, I went to Far Rockaway beach and filled a bottle with white sand. I thought of the years ahead for her. I remembered the graces of God numbered for Abraham: as many as the grains of sand and stars in the sky. I will you an hourglass of countless grains of white sand.

In Auschwitz death camp, I saw ashes of martyrs sifting through a large hourglass, running like a clock. I will you time, sifting both death and life slowly before your eyes, time moving, flowing, running. Time sifting as ocean sand through the eye of a needle.

I will you the motion of your watch, a clock, an hourglass emptying silently, refilling silently, not ticking, too soft for the ear to hear, running invisible before your eyes. I will you the unfolding of time, running before you like hidden tidal waves, moving higher, higher upon the shore, and then moving farther, farther into the sea. I will you the motion of time in March waking winter stems, in April waking ducklings, in May waking white roses. I will you seasons unfolding slowly as soft sand continuously running; seed barely moving, reaching, slowly ripening; blossoms buried in tight buds, breaking silently, wide-open, petals stretching boldly before the whole sky. I will you winter moving into spring. I will you the soft hands of the child, slowly moving into hands clasped in marriage, wrinkled softly by age, folded and clasped, holding, and then empty. I will you a long life. I will you the slow growing of your hands, your eyes, your mind, your spirit. I will you sights just ahead in a mountain climb, the vista inside an old word.

I will you an hourglass, emptying, turned over, and softly moving through summer to October into dim coloring of green oak leaves, the yellow of November willows, pecans falling, corn golden, and the white quilt of December. I will you the miracle of time moving, opening, flying, unfolding, climbing, falling, sleeping, waking, rising.

How do you feel the movement of time? Do you feel the quiet energy, mystic power, and glory of time? I will you the motion of time, the continuity of life, the quiet bursting of new seed. I will you one hourglass of thin ocean sand numbering the graces of God.

> *"I will surely do you good, and make your offspring*
> *as the sand of the sea, which cannot be counted*
> *because of their number." (Genesis 32:12)*

Swan Song

I will you fifty chapels underground in St. Mary's Cathedral. On Palm Sunday 1942, a firebomb found the cathedral. When planes were gone and ashes cold, only thick medieval walls stood. Music of once organists Buxtehude and Bach must have sobbed as the organs of St. Mary's in Luebeck burned. The bell towers flamed and bells started their way down from on high. People gasped in amazement, praying, staring at two burning spires.

I will you once feeling the fear and amazement, praying, and staring into a wartime fire. So on a Palm Sunday, a city faced incendiary flames and cried "Help, help; Hosanna." The donkey ride of Jesus is not over. Wood beams supporting three great bells burned through and two giant bells fell swinging, swaying, and dancing, in heat and fire to earth. It is said that swans sing a final tune before death. So, the bells in the sky sang a swan song as they tumbled. The city heard the hymn. Five hundred years of ringing sang a final tune.

You know the end of things, when the world watches a tower or a wall or a life tumble. You have witnessed it when a princess crashed, a Berlin wall broke, and two towers sank to the earth. I will you awe as bells and walls and towers dance and sing to their end of life. May your prayer be their swan song.

The bells in Luebeck lay half buried in the earth, on top of graves under the floor. Six years passed, and the bells lay in dust.

We were twenty young people from many countries and there to restore. Then came our digging, the sand, bricks, picks, shovels, wheelbarrows, steel bars, and levels. The cathedral would have another life. We were there to begin that life.

I will you to start another life when bells are down, the floor broken, and walls are leaning. Under the floor was the great surprise: old graves, quiet, decorated as chapels. Fire silenced the bells, warped grave plaques, and opened underground chapels. Under the cathedral floor, graves are rooms, each decorated with Easter, Christmas, Jesus, Calvary, and Resurrection. Under the silent bells are silent chapels decorated with color, icons, promise, and hope. I will you an awesome song of two falling bells, silent with fifty chapels of hope beneath them.

The swan song is not the final tune. I will you the tunes of life after death. There is music beyond the spheres.

Holy Incense

The aroma of lilacs is strong incense in May. You know the incense of summer rain falling, autumn leaves being raked, baked bread, fresh grain, and plowed earth. I will you the aroma of your mother by which you felt safe when newborn. I will you the incense of Mt. Olive church, the swinging censer, sparks bursting through fog, being caught in the cloud of God. I will you praying people who care about all senses, the smell of fresh apples, those who are poor, new sheep, a clean house, and candles burning.

I will you the incense of Mt. Olive, where we sat one Easter and all perfumes were extinguished by burning coals perfuming all worshipers the same. There was no difference between us and the homeless visitor two rows ahead. I will you the old secret, aroma, by which we knew mothers and fathers by heart, cried for them, and in their arms knew we were home. I will you old aromas that wait in you to be named, wrapped inside stories only you feel, sweet smelling incense, the beginning of icons only in your sensory album.

What are the aromas by which you feel you are home? Every home has its aroma. Open the door and you know it is your place. On a summer day the holy incense of Mt. Olive moves out into Chicago Avenue. I will you incense of all burnt offerings, perfuming any place to be holy.

I will you the incense of a candle on a cake, a carved pumpkin, a piece of toast, a cup of wine. Dark toast is a favorite toast, for the taste and the smell. For Lois, incense was often hot tea. I will you the aromas of nature that waken sacred emotions, God-given signs of hope and home.

Nathan's face was wet from crying. The room was full of people; he was lost. There was no comfort until he was in the arms of mother, his face into her skin. The perfume label spelled "Mama" and the baby was home. I pray that you find aromas to take you home.

"Perfume and incense make the heart glad." (Proverbs 27:9)

He Is Risen

"He is risen." This is how the story begins, and goes on and on. I will you a story with this profound beginning, "He is risen." That is the whole story in three words.

It was Easter Sunday, and we stood in church singing. My hymnal was open to the words, "Jesus Christ is risen today, Alleluia." I will you that grand fourteenth-century carol. The minister came from the altar up the aisle with a palm branch, a font basin, and water. Water splashed on us all, on some more and some less. A great shower came upon me and the hymn. I will you the shower of Easter rain while you sing. The thin pages of the Easter hymn soaked the droplets. The words "Jesus Christ is risen today" are wrinkled forever in this green hymnal. I felt the new book had been ruined. To the contrary. Number 151 is now the bookmark of that songbook. I will you hymn 151 in a green hymnal wrinkled with Easter water. I waited until the page dried. The page is no longer smooth. Hundreds will open a green hymnal to sing. Hymn 151 will open first. They may not know the reason. We do. This song has the name of the story I believe: "Jesus Christ is risen today." That is what I will you today: to believe in resurrection.

In the Middle Ages, water was poured into the font at Easter time. The baptized were dipped or washed with the water of Easter. They are buried with Christ and raised with Christ. Paul's writing to the Romans becomes alive when experienced this way.

People from a group home are members in our parish; one has brought her doll. She prays loudly what she knows by heart. When we say, "I believe in the resurrection," I look her way. Again, I am convinced, the way I was in my mother's lap, and in a seminary class titled, "The Life of Christ." Dr. Mattes, a tall professor with very white hair leaning over his podium was convincing when I was twenty, as convincing as the small woman from the group home now that I am eighty. Surely, you have found someone who says, "He is risen," and you believe. I bequeath you Easter water and someone who says, "He is risen—for sure."

Easter Nest

Have you made an Easter egg nest? Is the feeling of Easter still in you? I will you the thrill of shaping a nest hidden that is to be found. One made by hand with dried grass tangled, still cold from a long winter. A nest made of grass, soft leaves, or moss. A nest hidden where you must remember to find it in the morning. I will you a nest made of left-over leaves, new grasses, acorns, autumn blossoms crushed to make a sacred gentle place. I will you a nest made big as your own fist pressed expectantly into the center of a pile of raked grasses and very tiny twigs, placed behind a tree, under a bush, beneath a log, and in tall weeds, or under a chair, a table, a bed.

You know the feeling of hiding something and remembering where it is hidden, of having a secret and not forgetting the secret. Does your heart still race at Easter? What is there in the story that is childlike and never quits thrilling us? I will you running to see if Easter has come, the color of the eggs, printed messages, if a nest was missed, who brought the eggs. Were you proud of your secret nests? Did you show each to mother or father in case you forgot the hiding places? I will you someone you love who knows your hiding places. Easter was a glad day.

Remember the joy of a colored egg peeking through thin grass in a nest you hid? I will you the joy of spring, dead or plastic grass making a nest, Easter, the story of women looking for where Jesus was laid, and Mary finding him in a garden. I will you the miracle of glad days. Making a nest when I was a boy began a song in me I wrote sixty years later: "Alleluia, Jesus Is Risen."

Alleluia! Jesus is risen!
Trumpets resounding in glorious light!
Splendor, the Lamb, heaven forever!
Oh, what a miracle God has in sight!
Give God the glory! Alleluia!

Potter's Wheel

We saw Chris at his potter's wheel in our house. He held a lump of clay tight to the center of a turning disc, spinning like a merry-go-round, anchored, grounded, steady. Chris found the center where there was no wobble to the clay. I will you the quiet center, where all weight is balanced, and there is no wobble. I will you the quiet middle of a lump of potter's clay, waiting to unfold.

His hands held the outside of the whole lump, steady, ready to be formed, inside, outside. With one finger, the potter reaches into the center of the lump, both hands hold the circumference. I will you being formed at the center and circumference, at once, balanced.

His hands were steady: listening to the clay, finding the shape, strong inside and outside. His eyes were hopeful, eager, sure. I will you the hopeful eyes of a potter. What is it you shape and form? What is your lump of clay? The lump of clay began to rise, taller, wider; a vessel began to form.

The hands and the clay stayed in sync; the clay and the creator obeyed each other. I will you being in sync with the creator. Water, clay, the maker, the spinning wheel were in harmony. The vessel grew, centered, tall. There was no wobble. I will you a life balanced, wet, pliable, forming, upright.

Chris has a vision. He sees what this clay can be. His fingers spread, press, tighten. He makes a lip, a handle, a rim. The vessel he crafts is handmade, created. I will you the quietness of shaping a new creation: a pot, a casserole, a song, a child, a quilt, a new job, a family. Chris made it a vessel: for drink, food, violets, soup, crackers, wine, candles. The vessel is quiet as the spinning clay stands on its own, created. It was let go; it is his, mine, ours. How can this be? It was the hands; it was the clay. He listened to the clay. I call the vessel Sabbath, rest. I bequeath you to be centered, rested, balanced, at peace. We are connected, from deep within to all around.

> "O Lord . . . we are the clay, and you are our potter;
> we are all the work of your hand." (Isaiah 64:8)

New Song

How often have you taken fifty words and put them together as never before? This was your letter, song, memo, or poem. I bequeath you a brand-new song, words never so rhymed, for a tune never written. A sound never so made, and a feeling never so expressed. I will you a new song written in four lines, thirty-two, forty, fifty words, sung by a choir of two hundred voices, or by a friend in your house. I will you four lines written and hummed for the first time, with notes that no one has ever heard. I will you a new song, not yet born, barely being whispered, still silent, not yet on paper.

You make things that are new. You are known for doing something special, being unique, as different. What is it? It may not be a song. It is your own making.

I will you a song in the process of being born. Do you know the feeling? I will you the excitement of a new song: old words known from the beginning, adjectives and verbs linked as never before, never so said, and never so sung. I will you something so new it will have its own name you will give it. I will you a tune still a secret, still coming, soon to breathe its first sound, a surprise. I will you a new arrangement of twelve words with adjectives coloring the nouns, adverbs shading verbs, verbs soft and bursting and running. I will you the scrambling of words into a few lines of a new hymn, a hit, an anthem, a poem, a love note, a greeting card.

Find a new way to do an old thing.

Here are thirteen words, and a new song: "Winter snow blankets Mother Earth. Do you know who gave the snowflake birth?"

I will you the wonder of birthing a very new song never before written. I will you a soup of thirteen ingredients never so made. I bequeath you a list of thirteen thoughts never so made into a valentine. I bequeath you thirteen plants that make a new garden for a friend.

I write songs. My older brother helps people hoe gardens. You will find your new song. Fifty words give me a new song. Fifty minutes give my brother a new garden.

West

My favorite direction is west: the dusk, sunset, night, the evening star. I will you straight west: Mr. Otto's windmill against a night sky, and whirling slowly in a prairie sunset. In my childhood, west is a peaceful windmill putting to rest days of my youth. But, had I not known about the rising sun, I would have cried each night looking west into dusk and dark.

There is a direction you like facing. It may be set to the sun, time of day, a relative, friend, or a place you know well. Have you thought about west?

I will you west, where we watched clouds for rain to come, for rain to stop, for father to come home from Elk Creek up a long mud hill. West is where we took one gallon of cream each week to sell in the creamery next to the hardware store. I will you west where Loretta my teacher lived, with her parents and a brother, in a very tiny old house I felt was not good enough for her. What do you have that is in the west? Just west, near west, far west? West was Colorado where mother's father lived, where there were rivers and mountains I could find on a map, where I would go some day. West is where people homesteaded and trains began moving people along trails that oxen walked to make a path.

West was the side of church for the cemetery where all were buried so they would rise facing east toward the New Jerusalem. So west was about Easter and getting a new life. West is where mother planted rose moss on a grave we owned. From the west is where I walked miles in the dark, past barking dogs, bringing home dirty clothes in a bag from college. West is where I plowed my first straight row alone for Mr. Spilker, who bragged about it to farmers the next day.

What all is in west for you? I will you west where rain came fast and we would shut windows in the house to keep water off the floor. West is where the Mediterranean Sea was for St. Paul to set sail on his mission journeys. West is where Mark and Beth and Jon and Chris walked to climb a hill to school. I will you west that paints evening skies before dark. Find all that is west for you.

I will you west. Then east and south and north. West is in the song I practiced a hundred times when I was twelve and never learned to play, "Day Is Dying in the West," a song we harmonized in camps at dusk. I will you your own west, where every full day closes, light sleeps, and hope takes over.

"*The* LORD *speaks and summons the earth*
from the rising of the sun to its setting." (Psalm 50:1)

Heaven

Not a day has passed since childhood that I have not imagined heaven. The pictures do not stay the same. The early ones do not go away. The recent ones are not always the most comforting. Heaven is on my mind.

My friend John was the host of a radio program named, "Heaven Is in Your Mind." He sent me those words on a bumper sticker. I hung it by my desk and studied it for years. Slowly I began to understand. Heaven is indeed pictured in our minds. We redraw the pictures of Scripture to fit our spirit. My early pictures were much like my early life in Nebraska. Heaven was dear family and friends. There were other adults and children, but their faces were dim. Then I was a child, now I am an adult. My heaven picture has changed, but it's still familial and homey. My roots are the country.

The book of Revelation paints the picture of a city, the New Jerusalem. This picture came alive as I sang hymns about this holy city, especially, "Jerusalem the Golden." Gold and glistening and light and rubies were in that picture of heaven. It was elegant, beyond what we knew in our country household. It was more like my mother's jewelry drawer. I will you a heaven that is familial, elegant, and golden.

A nun and I wrote many books together. Glistening light and reflection were important in these books. Her photos often glowed. She saw heaven as light and beauty. She repeated the words of Revelation and heaven and added: "If you want heaven more beautiful, see it more beautiful. God wants you to make it as pretty as you can." So, my childhood picture took on color and glamour.

Later, I visited the island of Patmos, where John had the vision of heaven described in Revelation. One sunset on the sea of Patmos showed me John's view of the city of gold and jewels. My picture of heaven became even more beautiful. I saw the holy city in a sunset.

Old loved ones have passed away. My grandson Henry went as an infant. I see rocking chairs in the city of gold, some holding mothers humming to babies, some holding old friends; and I see children dressed in garments of light. Musical friends have passed, and now the sounds of heaven are brighter, the vibrations of instruments and heaven's harmony have increased.

Some say the dead are asleep in heaven, they will wake later. I look at my watch and think of "now" and "later." God's time is another time, eternal time. There is no now and later in God's time. In heaven, there will be a new form, new body, spiritual body. I am in awe. Silent. Believing.

I wish I knew your pictures of heaven. You have some of mine. I bequeath you my beautiful view of heaven. I will you a sweet foretaste of heaven.

Omni

When I was seven, I learned three words in church school that I did not understand but loved dearly: omniscient, omnipotent, omnipresent. My father said I would grow to understand these words. This year I have learned to understand the *omni* part of the words. I will you *omni*.

I did know then that *omni* was what God knew and did. *Omni* was like saying "all"—all-wise, all-powerful, all-present. I have lived in awe of this all-ness of God. It has been a great comfort to know that I do not and cannot live in the world of *omni*. Not now, maybe never. The lines that divide *omni* from "present," "power," and "wise" are clear and sharp. I am in a world of limits: limited space, limited power, limited wisdom. I cannot know that greater space out there or in myself. As friends grew in years and faced hurt and death, my world of limits bumped into *omni* more than before. Recently, a film-maker's wife died. He had for years looked into the world through a lens. Always, he could find his subject: castle, tree, blossom, caterpillar, face. When his wife died, he phoned to ask: "Now how will I find her?" His wife is in the *omni* world. I mentioned this to a friend. She said, "Love will help him find her." Love works in the *omni* world. A camera will not.

After fifty-four years of marriage, my wife Lois died last July. The *omni* world opened wider for me. In the dark of that world, I feel and see and hear what is printed in Scripture. I am drawn into a world bigger than the present and into a strength greater than any power on earth, into an understanding far beyond my own.

I will you God's omnipotence and omnipresence and omniscience. I will you space and time beyond the present, a world bigger than the globe or universe. You can look beyond what you see. I will you eyes to see and ears to hear and mind to know the mind of Christ, the wonder of beyond. The wonder of deep inside. The wonder of the Alpha and Omega. The wonder of the spirit, the soul, the whole story of salvation. I will you the silence of *omni*, its rhythm, music, mystery, holiness. I will you a glimpse of *all*.

Good-bye

"Good-bye," we say; "God be with you," we are saying.

I feel the power of good-bye. I remember the sight of waving hands from buses on choir tours, hands filling the windows with blurred fingers. I remember handkerchiefs flying until we were out of sight in the days of visiting Iron Curtain countries. Good-bye is a power. Feel the warmth of a good-bye hug, being held by a dear friend, a dad or mom—a recent hug or one long ago. I will you "Good-bye, Mom." I will you the look in the eyes when saying good-bye one more time, and another, and another. I will you the hug that may be the last hug, the wave that may be the final wave; you do not know. The sound of "I love you" hangs in the silent air as you leave the room, the hospital, the prison.

And there is a good-bye to things we love. There is the good-bye to seasons: no more summer, no more falling leaves. Now it is winter, now it is cold. Silent roots in the earth wait for April. I will you good-bye to a tree you loved long, now with a red line painted around its trunk; good-bye to a house you know by heart; good-bye to a job you once could do so easily; good-bye to a mountain you will not climb again.

I will you good-bye with laughter, a shout, a clapping of hands, the joyful end of a good time. I will you a good-bye that looks for the next time, and the next. I will you the good-bye that hollers, "Call me. Write. E-mail me. I'll be back." There is the good-bye that does not need to turn back to look, the good-bye that will stand and wait, pray, give thanks, smile inside. There is room in you for good-bye that shouts and echoes, that always thinks of another time—if not here, in heaven. "See you in heaven" is a saying both old and fresh. Good-bye is never final; there always will be another time. I will you good-bye filled with song: "God be with you 'til we meet again."

The maple tree is silent, the snow upon each stem;
There is a sleep so silent we know not why or when.

The maple tree is silent; gold leaves are 'neath the snow,
and if we watch the maple, we know where winters go.

The maple tree is silent; it is more still than still,
The leaves will soon be budding; I know they will, they will.